Tales from Thailand

as told by Marian Davies Toth
illustrated by Supee Pasutanavin

CHARLES E. TUTTLE COMPANY
Rutland · Vermont & Tokyo · Japan

Table of Contents

7

four sons and I flew across the Pacific Ocean to meet my husband in Bangkok, Thailand. Our jet flew high enough for us to see night chase dawn across the Pacific. Fortunately, our plane was not punctured by a star, so we landed smoothly at Don Muang Airport. The next day it seemed as if I had returned to that dream of long ago, for I saw a little girl flying a lovely yellow kite as she stood next to a giant red swing in the center of Bangkok.

During my entire stay in Thailand, or Siam as it was once known, I had a strange sensation, as if I had not completely awakened from a dream. Thailand does have an elusive, dreamlike quality that inspires one to search for origins and touchstones of reality. In the Thai legends, folktales, and myths, I discovered the Thai had attempted to explain life as they had understood it. Some of their stories told of how things came to be, others illustrated the behavior of man in all his inexplicable diversity. All these stories have been described and inscribed in the minds of successive generations of Thai.

The stories presented in this collection are authentic Thai tales; however, paragraphs of description and explanatory comments have been woven into the stories in order to clarify plot and meaning. One story, "The Tale of the Ricebirds," is told in Thailand, but it is of

Indian origin. The author believes this representation of Indian influence is appropriate because numerous Indian stories have fused into the fabric of the folklore of Thailand.

This book contains a selection of the most suitable children's stories from a collection of one hundred original Thai tales. Some of the stories have never been recorded prior to this time. These stories came from the elder Thai who remembered them from their childhood. In each instance a special effort has been made to maintain the original character of the story. The result of my research is this collection of stories which attempts to preserve a portion of the living folklore of Thailand. It is my sincere hope that this book will provide a glimpse of Thailand as seen through the eyes of a Thai.

MARIAN DAVIES TOTH

of Bangkok's famous International School. Her sincere enthusiasm and her recognition of the need for a children's book of Thai folklore encouraged its creation. I also wish to thank my International School students who had an insatiable appetite for stories. Additionally, I am grateful to Mrs. Patrick G. Wardell for her capable secretarial assistance.

During the development of this book I benefited greatly from the guidance provided by Tuak Kusuma, Thailand's foremost authority on Thai folklore. Mr. Kusuma presently teaches folklore at Chulalongkorn University and Prosom Mit, Bangkok's Graduate School of Education. He edited the book to preserve the distinct Thai individuality of each story and patiently monitored each story to assure its authenticity in fact and substance. Several stories were included in this collection at his suggestion.

My sincere appreciation is extended to my friend and teacher of creative writing, Dr. J. Wesely Ingles, and I wish to thank Dr. Dan Ben-Amos, School of Folklore and Folklife, University of Pennsylvania, for his suggestions on future folklore projects. I am grateful to Dr. Ward Hunt Goodenough, School of Anthropology, University of Pennsylvania, for his stimulating lectures in cultural anthropology which revealed the enormous potential of the folktale as an ethnographic tool.

Mrs. Valai Leelanuj and my numerous Thai friends generously answered a myriad of questions. For their patience and consideration, and for the help of all who made this collection of tales a reality, I am truly grateful.

PART ONE

Stories of Old Siam

HOW-IT-CAME-TO-BE STORIES

1. How the Bay of Siam Came to Be

Once upon a time a kite flew above yellow bamboo roof-tops, past green jungles, and high into the bright blue sky of Siam. During the day it blocked the sun from sight, and at night it hid the moon. This kite was larger than a tiger, larger than an elephant, larger than a house. It was the largest kite in Siam, and it may have been the largest kite in the world.

If you slid from the kite through clouds and down the long yellow jute rope that served as a kite string, you would find yourself in the compound of Khun Keha. He was the most original and the most clever kite maker in Siam. Khun Keha was an old man, but he always felt young when kites were flying. During the third month of the waning moon, the mango monsoons from the east blew like gusts from a giant bamboo fan. The largest kite in Siam needed strong winds to keep it flying. Khun Keha prayed to the gods to encourage the winds to blow. He had spent over a year making his gigantic masterpiece, and now he hoped all the children in his village would be able to enjoy it.

The great idea for the kite came in the Year of the Snake on a day when Khun Keha's compound hummed with the busy noises of children making kites. Saws sang, frames rattled, and glue-soaked rice paper flapped. Sawdust puffed into the air like the pollen of flowers. Paint brushes swished reds, blues, and yellows over slender strips of bamboo. Khun Keha could not take a step without meeting a question.

"Is it true that kites can call the winds and bring rain to the rice field, Khun Keha?"

"*Chai,* it is so. Kites have done this. Kites can even tell what will happen in the future. Some wise men look at a flying kite and see in each motion a glimpse of things to come."

"Can kites do anything else, Khun Keha?"

"*Chai,*" he answered, "sometimes we use them to carry explosive bombs to the enemy. Kites are good soldiers."

"Khun Keha, could a man ride in a kite?" asked a child.

With the asking of this question, Khun Keha paused and shook his head. "*Mai ruu,* I don't know," he replied. "No one has ever tried it. I guess a man would have to build a kite almost as big as a house in order to ride in it."

"Could you build a kite that big?" they asked.

Khun Keha laughed and said, "I don't know, but I guess I could try. Will you help me?"

The children shouted, *"Chai!"* and shrieked with delight at the thought of having a kite as big as a house.

"Run along now, children. We will think about it, but you must rest now. Tomorrow is the day when we watch the kite fights."

The day ran after the night, and the next day Khun Keha took his little friends to watch the kite fights in the parade ground stretching in front of the king's royal palace.

"Watch carefully, children, the kites are like boys and girls quarreling. The male kites are called *chula* kites. They are big and star shaped. The female kites are called *pakpao*. They are small and dainty.

"Kite fighting is a team sport. The object is to get your kite into the air, keep it flying, yet handle it with care and guide it into attacks upon the enemy kite. Both the *chula* and the *pakpao* try to force each other out of the sky."

After the kite fight he took the children home and taught them how to make *chula* and *pakpao* kites. His compound was full of laughter and the music of happy children.

"Where do I place the hooks on my *chula* kite?" a little boy asked.

"Put the hooks on the bottom so they can catch the strings of the *pakpao*," he said.

The little girls said, "Khun Keha, you want the *chula* kites to win! Come, help us with our *pakpao* kites."

"Now, children," Khun Keha comforted, "it isn't who wins that matters as much as how well one observes the rules of the game. In kite fighting there are fifty rules to remember. It takes a long time to learn all of them. Most of all, you must be as clever as a tiger when you fly the kites. You can make your *pakpao* twist and dip. Each flutter of wind sends the *pakpao* in unpredictable directions. The *pakpao* is like a chicken chased by a dog. You never know which way the chicken will go."

"*Chula* kites are stronger," said the boys.

"*Chai,*" said Khun Keha.

The little boys gathered around Khun Keha and said, "Khun Keha, why don't you make a *chula* kite that is bigger than a house?"

"We shall see, we shall see," he said.

When the official kite season was over, Khun Keha began to make an intricate *chula* kite. In order to make it long enough he had to remove the end of his house. To give the kite the proper height, he had to remove the ceiling from his house. Then, in order to add the sides, he had to tear down the remainder of the house. Poor Khun Keha did not have a house any more, but he had a kite, a giant kite. It was the only kite in Siam that was bigger than a house.

Every day the children came to watch Khun Keha paint swirls, diamonds, and intricate Siamese designs upon the kite. They agreed it was not only the largest but also the most beautiful kite in Siam.

On the first day of the waning moon in the Year of the Horse, the winds roared across the ocean and swept over the jungles into Siam. It was strong and steady wind. Before the sun dawned, all the children of the village assembled by Khun Keha's kite. They greeted their friend by clasping both hands together, bowing their heads, and saying, "*Sawaddi,* good morning, Khun Keha. Please, may we fly the kite today?"

Khun Keha smiled, "When a baby stands alone, we say he is setting up the egg. Today let us set up the egg for our kite and let it fly for the first time."

The children and Khun Keha took burning incense, flowers, and a serving of fresh rice to the little shrine, honoring the spirit of Khun Keha's compound. They knelt and asked the blessing of the gods upon the giant kite.

Khun Keha called eight of the larger children and gave each a heavy rope that was attached to the kite. He led by pulling the first rope himself. For a brief moment, no longer than it takes a *chingchok*, or lizard, to catch a fly, the kite seemed dead, but in the full force of the gale the kite was stirred to life. It soared into the sky like a giant bird. Higher and higher it flew while the children cheered and shouted.

When the kite was successfully launched, Khun Keha tied the long jute guide rope to a huge boulder. He spent the remainder of the day preparing the best surprise for the children. It was a sliding pulley that allowed the children to ride from the ground through the sky to the giant *chula* kite.

The children's faces brimmed with wonder as they floated in the kite with old Khun Keha. It was like being in a magical world. All around them were soft white clouds fleeced with silver. The only sound was the flap of a bird's wing or a whistle of wind. At this great height the wind only tickled the kite and made it sway like a swing. Far below them the earth seemed as neat as a Siamese chessboard with the rice paddies squarely marked. The network of *klong* looked like silver footpaths instead of waterways. All houses in the village looked the same, like little boxes on stilts with yellow roofs.

Each day during the kite season the children dashed home from school and then met Khun Keha in the clouds. He told them stories, gave them coconut candy, and celebrated the festive days. If he had not done these kind things, they still would have come because the greatest joy of all was observing the beauty of the world from the kite in the sky.

One day the clouds were dark and the skies were scowling. Khun Keha said, "A great storm is coming. You may not go up to the kite today."

As he spoke, harsh winds almost blew the children off their feet. The kite began to sway and its rock anchor moved slightly. "I fear our kite may be damaged in this storm. Let's bring it down."

Khun Keha and all the children pulled on the sturdy jute rope, but the force of the wind was so great that it lifted them from the ground. "*Rawang! Rawang!* careful, children. We must let the kite go!"

The children obeyed instantly, and just in time, for a powerful gust of wind carried their enormous kite high into the sky, so quickly that it disappeared from view before the children could catch their breath.

Khun Keha sent the children home while he prayed for the gods to return his kite.

What happened to the beautiful kite? What happened to the largest kite in Siam? We shall never know for certain, but the people who live in Southern Siam say that long ago a kite bigger than a house whirled through the sky, fell with a crash, tore open the earth, and created the Bay of Siam.

Now Khun Keha did not have a house, he did not have a kite, but he had the honor of changing the geography of his country, and he had the love of all the children in the village. He considered himself a wealthy man.

2. How the Mekong River Came to Be

Long ago, when the world was new, there were no rivers in old Siam. The gods had created streams, brooks, ponds, and pools, but no rivers ran from the mountains to the plains and from the plains to the China Sea. Five orphaned brothers lived in this riverless land. Their home was in the northern part of Siam where the mountains reach into the sky, where the air is crisp, and where a cool breeze flutters. Their only neighbors were forest animals such as plump bears, sleek tigers, and slithering cobra snakes. Birds with shrill tones and brilliant feathers sang mocking songs for the brothers. Rabbits and porcupines scurried on the forest floor. Herds of wild elephants roamed in the teak forests surrounding their bamboo hut.

These boys were hunters, masters of the crossbow. With their sharp bamboo arrows and strong teakwood bows they were able to slay swift-running deer. They could bring down flying swallows. Even the tigers were not safe when the five brothers hunted. The youngest brother, Mekong, was the best hunter of the group. It has been said that he was able to pierce the eye of an eagle as it soared through the clouds.

The brothers were jealous of Mekong, jealous of one another, and as a result they quarreled and fought like bear cubs. Ping and Wang, the eldest brothers, often accused Yom and Nan, the younger brothers, of not sharing their game with them. Then there were times when Yom and Nan accused Ping and Wang of telling untruths about their hunting gains.

Once, Nan said, "Ping, you and Wang wrap your tongue around your ears. You eat the fleshy parts of your catch, bring home the lean parts for us and say, 'This is all we killed today.' "

Wang laughed and said, "Who knows, you may be right little brother. I suspect that you do the very same thing."

One day the four older brothers went hunting, but they did not kill a single animal. No one knew the reason why the arrows missed their mark. Wang said his arrows were not sharp enough, Ping said his bowstring was not tight enough, Yom said his bow was not sturdy enough, and Nan said his eyes were blurry so he could not aim well enough. The four brothers returned home tired and weary, but imagine their delight when they saw Mekong roasting the carcass of a deer upon a spit above the open fire.

The brothers ate heartily and soon they were in a jovial mood.

Ping said, "Brothers, we should not quarrel as often as

we do. We should not also fight about the game we catch."

The other four brothers agreed, "*Chai, chai, chai, chai,* yes, yes, yes, yes!"

"We should share and share alike," said Yom.

"Why don't we do just that? Why, we could make a code, a code of the five brothers," said Wang excitedly.

"This idea, like the spring blossoms, brings me pleasure," said Mekong.

The embers in the fire sifted into ashes as the brothers discussed their code. Finally, it was agreed that each brother must bring home all the meat from every animal he killed. As a measure of proof, each brother also agreed to bring home something to identify his game.

"When I kill a deer, I'll bring home its meat and its antlers," said Nan.

"When I kill a bear, I'll bring you its meat, its tail, and claws," said Yom.

"If I ever kill an elephant, I'll bring my brothers its tusks," laughed Wang.

"My brothers," said Mekong, "you've given me hope. Our friendship was dying as grass dies when it is tread upon. Now, new hope springs like a fresh shoot of pale green. We are starting on a new path of respect and concern for one another."

Not long after this meeting Mekong was alone in the forest when he saw a small porcupine nibbling upon the bark of a tree. Before the porcupine noticed him, Mekong aimed his crossbow. His arrow pierced the quill coat of the porcupine, and the little animal died instantly. Mekong

quickly skinned it and discovered that he had killed a very small porcupine. His mouth watered, for porcupine meat is delicious. Mekong was tempted to build a fire, roast the porcupine, and eat it immediately; however, he remembered the code of the five brothers and returned home to share his small prize.

Unfortunately, on this very day, Wang, Yom, Ping, and Nan had been unsuccessful in their hunting. By the time they reached home they were hungry enough to eat the bark of a tree.

"Don't worry," said Ping. "Mekong will bring home something that is delicious."

"Perhaps, he will bring home another deer."

"I hope he has caught twenty rabbits."

"My mouth waters for bear meat."

Finally, Mekong arrived with the tiny portion of porcupine meat, nothing else.

Wang said, "Mekong, you must be joking. This is not a complete animal. Please, explain your miserable offering!"

Mekong tried to defend himself, "Brothers, you are mistaken. It is a whole animal. It is the only thing I killed today. I am as hungry as you are. I was tempted to eat all the meat myself, but I brought it home to share with you."

The brothers stared at Mekong. They were convinced that he was trying to cheat them. When they demanded proof of the animal's identity, Mekong poured a large bag of porcupine quills upon the floor. As the brothers gazed at the multitude of quills, they were further convinced that the animal must have been larger.

The gods in heaven were disturbed by the loud shouts and screams of violent anger. They listened as the brothers shouted, "Mekong, leave our home and never come back. There is no place here for one who cheats."

Mekong brushed the tears from his eyes, picked up his crossbow, and left without saying another word.

The gods were horrified at the rash, uncontrollable tempers of Wang, Ping, Yom, and Nan. "They must be punished for treating Mekong so unfairly," one god declared.

"Ah! yes, and Mekong must be rewarded for remaining loyal to the code of the five brothers," cried another.

"Wait," said the first god, "let us not reward and punish now. Let us watch over Mekong. This is not an easy matter to decide. If we wait for the waxing and the waning of the moon, we shall be better prepared to judge fairly."

Mekong never returned to his home in the high hills. He wandered through the eastern part of Siam and finally traveled south, past the Central Plain, and all the way to the China Sea.

After many lunar years the gods decided that all five brothers should be turned into rivers. Mekong was honored and his name was given eternal life when the gods transformed him into the largest river in Siam. The Mekong River follows the route of his lonely journey. The four ill-tempered brothers achieved fame of a lesser kind. Their hunting paths became the beds of the Ping, Wang, Yom, and Nan rivers. Now and forever more, these four small rivers ripple over the winding hunting trails used by the four harsh brothers long, long ago when the world was new.

3. How the Fire Festival Came to Be

The people in northeast Thailand worship an ancient god of Indian origin called Phya Tan. He is so powerful that he can destroy the earth at will. When the northeast hilltribes observe their crops turning brown with drought or watch their homes float away in floods, they interpret the catastrophes as acts of vengeance from their angry god. Their soil produces the poorest crops in Thailand, yet the people never give up hope that some day Phya Tan will give them a bountiful harvest and prosperity.

Each spring the northeastern Thai celebrate the Bong Fire Festival in honor of Phya Tan. They show their appreciation for his goodness in a colorful, noisy ritual held in the sweetly scented temple gardens where the air is heavy with the fragrance of flowering jasmine and burning incense. The following story tells how the Bong Fire Festival began. It also explains how gods came to earth from heaven and became the earliest ancestors of the Thai.

*   *   *

Phya Tan, the God of the World, looked down from the sky at his people. "All I see is sin!" he said. He watched a little boy steal a sweet mango from an old woman's basket. He heard children speaking rudely to their parents. The parents shouted insults at the children and to one another. A friend refused his companion's request for the loan of five silver *tical*.

"The most noble virtues have been forgotten. The fathers do not love their sons. The sons do not do their parental duties. Between husband and wife there is no kindness and obedience. The young do not respect the old. Friends do not keep faith with one another. Ah! Man is no better than beast. The earth must be destroyed," said Phya Tan.

As Phya Tan spoke, hungry flames blazed through the sky and raced over the earth. The seas boiled until mighty waves spurted frothy white streams into the sky. All the fish lost their lives. The water in the vast rice fields began to steam. Rice plants quickly wilted and died as a blanket of intense heat enclosed the earth and extinguished the life of everything on the surface.

Winds carried the smells of the burning earth to heaven where Sang Kasa and Sang Kasi, two children of the gods, looked down upon the blazing ball of fire.

"Hmmm, what a wonderful odor!" said Sang Kasi. "I smell roasting fowl, boiled fish, and sweet fruits."

"Let's go to that strange place called earth and see what's happening," said Sang Kasa.

The two inquisitive children made a jute rope ladder and at dusk they descended from heaven to earth. When they arrived, they sat upon the blackened ground and ran their fingers through the soil. Sang Kasi picked up a handful of black earth, smelled it, and then tasted it.

He called to Sang Kasa, "Taste this good earth. It's like a strange rice."

"There really isn't anything else to eat," answered Sang Kasa. She placed a tiny morsel on her tongue and to her great surprise she discovered the scorched earth was delicious.

As they consumed this strange dinner, the little boy and girl gods experienced an unusual sensation. With each bite of earth they lost a memory of their previous life. They also lost the magical powers that only the gods possess. Their wings disappeared so they could not fly. Their eyes lost the magical vision so they could no longer see great distances. The children were unaware of the gradual change and continued eating until they had become human beings. Now their needs and weaknesses were like those of the earth people.

Far beyond the open face of the sky sat Phya Tan, observing the runaways.

"Sang Kasa and Sang Kasi are children of the gods. Perhaps they can bring the noble virtues back to the earth," he said.

With this thought in mind, he banished Sang Kasa and Sang Kasi forever as he ripped their jute ladder to shreds. Now there was no possible way for the children to return to heaven, so they were forced to make a home on earth.

For many moons the earth was a desolate place. There was no sun, no morning, and no noon. No dawn and no dusk marked the rise and rest of a passing day. And then, it is said, Phya Tan took pity on the children and sent cool rains to moisten the earth. Once again he allowed the sun to spill golden light upon the earth and coax grass, plants, and trees back to life. The old earth became fresh again with the smells of spring, moist earth, and growing plants. With the help of Phya Tan the wounds of the great fire healed and eventually a new cycle of life was re-established.

Sang Kasa and Sang Kasi married and became the proud parents of many children. They lived long enough to see their children marry and even held their great-grandchildren upon their laps. Their descendants eventually learned how to build bamboo huts, cultivate rice crops, and build nets for catching fish. They prospered because Phya Tan smiled upon them. The sun shone brightly and the rains fell gently when the plants needed nourishment. There was no drought and no floods rushed over the land.

One day Phya Tan watched the earth people harvest a rice crop that would provide food in the pot for everyone. He saw that all the earthmen found fishes in their nets. Yellow and red bananas, sweet papayas, the cheeselike durian, and the delicious, peach-tasting mangoes were to be had for the plucking.

"I have been good to these people, but they never think of their god," said Phya Tan. "If I hide the rain clouds, I will teach them a lesson in humility."

That year the green rice sprouts raised their heads, but turned brown and withered for there was no rain. As the drought continued, the fruits became wrinkled and hard like stones. The streams disappeared into a dry, thirsty soil. The waterfalls ceased flowing and many people died from thirst and hunger. But a strange thing happened. It is said that those who survived were changed somehow.

The fathers showed love for their sons, and the sons responded with a new respect for their fathers. Husbands treated their wives with a new kindness, and the wives obeyed their husband's requests. Friends kept faith with one another and gladly shared the little they possessed. The great drought had made the people considerate of one another. They became better than beasts. They became thinking men.

One day the survivors sat together sharing a few scraps of food.

"We must thank the great Phya Tan for our lives," said the elder of the group.

"We must send Phya Tan a message of love," said his wife.

"Perhaps, if he knows we are grateful for life, he will send rain," said a priest.

"*Chai, chai,* yes, yes," the others agreed.

The people talked excitedly and, it is said, that from this meeting a great plan was made. The people decided to show Phya Tan they appreciated life, loved one another, and were sorry for not thanking him when their lives had been rich with his bountiful gifts.

The next day they gathered golden bamboo trees and filled the hollow trunks with a powerful, explosive powder. The women plucked poinsettias and *mali*, the sweet-smelling jasmine. The priests brought candles and incense. All morning long the people decorated the rockets until they were suitable for the eyes of their god.

When everything was ready the survivors assembled by

their *wat*, or temple. All was silent except for the tinkling rings of the little bronze bells dangling from the rafters of the temple roof. Incense misted the air with its sweet fragrance. The people bowed to heaven, then lay prostrate upon the hard ground. Their lips muttered prayers and requests for forgiveness.

The saffron-robed priests carried flaming torches to the base of the bamboo rockets. The fire ignited the powder and the rockets began to sputter, sizzle, and slowly rise into heaven. The beautiful, blazing bamboos sparked like flashes of lightning in the sky. As Phya Tan witnessed this unusual spectacle and heard the prayers of his people, his heart was made happy. It was now evident that the earth people had learned the beauty of the noble virtues.

It is said that a gentle shower of rain fell that day. The people danced in the rain drops, sang happy songs, and shouted with gladness. Each splash of welcome rain was a message from Phya Tan telling them of his love and forgiveness.

Every year from that time until this, the people of northeast Thailand have saved a warm May day to honor Phya Tan with the Bong Fire Festival. During the celebration troubles disappear and happiness reigns. Phya Tan is shown gratitude, and his people are given encouragement for a prosperous year, made richer with an awareness of the noble virtues.

4. How Thunder and Lightning Came to Be

When lightning flashes and thunder roars, the Thai mothers say, "Don't be afraid, my children. It's only Mekhala flashing her crystal jewel. She is teasing the cruel god of thunder, Ramasura."

Mekhala is a beautiful Thai goddess with sparkling black eyes and shining black hair. It is said she was born in the foam of the sea. She is the goddess of the streams, rivers, and oceans of the world.

Ramasura is the demigod, half ogre and half divine. He wears a green suit and carries a beautiful ax decorated with diamonds. He was born in a storm cloud, and to this day he wears the rain cloud as a cloak.

All the gods and goddesses are fond of Mekhala because of her happy, carefree manner. They delight in watching her tease those who are serious. Her favorite victim is Ramasura. He is not a popular god because, it is said, he is harsh, cruel, and impetuous. Worst of all, he has a very bad habit of throwing his ax at those who offend him. Fortunately, Ramasura and Mekhala do not meet very often. During most of the year Mekhala is confined to Siva's palace where she spends all her time polishing her crystal jewel.

When Mekhala became of marriageable age, her father presented her to the great god Siva.

"Now Mekhala, you must be a good wife to Siva," he said. "My wedding gift to you is a sparkling crystal jewel. It will amuse you and keep you occupied. You must always keep it polished, my child."

"Chai," said Mekhala. "I shall do as you say, father."

She tried to keep her word, and she did, indeed, polish her crystal ball until it sparkled as brightly as the most brilliant star. But polishing the jewel was Mekhala's only task, and soon she became bored with her work.

"If I only had someone to talk to," she sighed. "I do wish Siva did not leave me alone in this beautiful floating palace."

One day, when the rainy season began, the gods and goddesses assembled in their heaven and celebrated the life-giving gift of rain. They sang and danced as happily as mortals. Since it was such a special occasion, Siva allowed Mekhala to attend the party. The moment she arrived, everyone stopped dancing and looked at her sparkling eyes, shining hair, and her beautiful crystal jewel that flashed beams of light into the sky.

When Ramasura saw the beautiful Mekhala he walked toward her. She flashed her jewel in his eyes and laughed at the huge god.

"Don't you know who I am?" he roared.

Mekhala giggled and flew in and out of the fluffy clouds.

The winds howled and whipped through the sky as Ramasura tried to find Mekhala. Most goddesses would have been terrified, but not Mekhala. She thought it was great fun to hide in the clouds and spark her jewel at Ramasura. She led him all over heaven as she skipped and giggled, diving into clouds and hiding in their mists. The more she laughed, the more enraged Ramasura became.

"I'll catch that little teaser, if it is the last thing I do," he said.

No one could catch a goddess who darted as fast as a flash of sunlight, and it appeared as if Mekhala had escaped from Ramasura. Then, all of a sudden, he raised his arm and aimed his glittering ax at Mekhala. She flashed her crystal in his eyes and blinded him just as the ax flew from his hand with a thunderous roar. Time and time again he hurled his ax at her, but his aim was always spoiled by the light from her jewel.

On a stormy night when the sky is gray, look into the sky. That flash of lightning is the sparkle of Mekhala's crystal jewel. The roar of thunder is Ramasura's ax rolling across the corridors of the sky. If you sit very still and listen carefully you may hear Mekhala's tinkling laughter, and if the clouds should part suddenly, you may see a graceful goddess darting above the mists with a sparkling crystal jewel flashing rays of brilliant light into Ramasura's angry eyes.

5. How the Thai Learned to Be Calm

Once there was a village, a quiet, sleepy village. It was called Peaceful Village because everyone who lived there said, "My neighbor is my friend." There the people worked together each season of the year. In the rain, in the heat, in the dry, cool air, they were always together like bunches of bananas in a tree. Then one day a terrible thing happened as quickly and unexpectedly as a flash of lightning in the sky. Peace left the village, and loving neighbors became enemies.

It happened one day long, long ago when the red sun burned over the horizon and shone on the bamboo huts in Peaceful Village. The roosters crowed, as they always did, and stretched their wings like unfolding fans. The pigs oinked and poked their noses in the earth under the houses. The rice farmers washed the sleep from their eyes, rinsed their mouths with fresh water, and chewed a wad of betel nut before going to work in the paddy. The women hastened to put yokes on the water buffaloes and awaken their sleepy sons. The boys rode on the backs of the buffaloes and guided them to the paddy.

That morning a little *chingchok,* no bigger than a mouse, slithered onto the dirt road running through the center of Peaceful Village. Its gray lizard body looked like a drop of mud slung from the hoof of a buffalo. The farmers and their sons passed the *chingchok* on the way to their work in the paddy. The shopkeeper's sons skipped by it on their way to the *wat* where they recited their lesson for the priest. No one paid any attention to this *chingchok* because others just like him were in the houses, the trees, and in the compounds of every Thai family.

The *chingchok* ignored the morning traffic and fell fast asleep by the side of the road. Nothing disturbed him, not even the little boy who returned home from a honey hunt with the cones of the wild *pung* bee dangling from a stick held over his shoulder. As he skipped down the road, his sweet bundle swayed, and a golden drop of honey flew through the air, landing on the sand beside the sleeping *chingchok.* The honey gleamed in the hot sun.

This day, long ago, seemed like any other day. The lizard slept, the honey sparkled, and the housewives went on with their work. They cooked the morning rice, scooped it on banana leaves, and wrapped it like a present with a rattan string. The children carried the little green bundles to their fathers in the paddy. Some wives mashed rice into flour with mortar and pestle. Others wove cotton threads into fabric on large handlooms.

In one compound, not far from the sleeping *chingchok*, a woman and her friend swung a little baby to sleep in a cradle.

> The crocodile in yonder tree
> Looks fierce beyond belief.
> You need not Yim,
> Be scared of him,
> He hasn't any teeth.

The baby gurgled. His mother rocked him and sang:

> It's twelve o'clock my baby,
> The turtle dove is still;
> He cries from dawn to noon time
> But now his voice is still,
> And you must rest, my baby,
> For the sun is past the hill.

When the baby fell fast asleep, his mother said to her friend, "Today I saw two *chingchok* fighting on the wall of our hut."

"It is an omen of evil. You know it means your family will suffer illness and maybe death," said the woman as her face wrinkled into a worried frown.

"You must give the guardian spirit of your place an offering of rice. If you burn incense for him and bring him fresh flowers, he may keep the evil from falling upon you."

"*Chai*, yes, we must do everything possible to send the evil away."

Two little children, a boy and a girl, listened to their mothers' conversation.

Thai Learned to Be Calm **43**

"Run along, little rat, run along, little rabbit," the mothers said to them. The children skipped down the road arm in arm.

"My mother is terribly worried because the *chingchok* battled on the wall of our house this morning," said the little girl.

"Ah, it is a very bad omen," said the little boy.

As they passed the sleeping *chingchok*, the little girl said, "Look, this *chingchok* sleeps just an elephant's step away from my cat."

"And my dog is sleeping in the shade behind your cat," said the little boy.

Just then the *chingchok* opened his beady eyes. The first thing he saw was the drop of honey gleaming in the sunlight. With a fast dart and one quick lick of his tongue he devoured the honey. The scurry of the *chingchok* alerted the cat. She caught him with her paw and rolled him over in the sand. The scuffle awakened the dog. He snarled and barked at the cat. She arched her back and hissed like the fuse on a fire cracker. The dog growled fiercely.

The girl grabbed a stick and beat the snapping dog.

"Don't you dare hurt my cat," she said.

The little boy began to beat the little girl and he shouted, "Don't you dare hurt my dog!"

The girl's mother came running to the scene. She slapped the boy and screamed, "Don't you dare hurt my little girl."

The boy's mother heard him cry and rushed to the street.

"You beast," she yelled, "don't you dare hurt my little boy."

Friends of both women came running. When they heard the story, they plunged into the fight, throwing sticks and stones, and shouting vile insults. The women even pointed their toes at their enemies' heads. Nothing was more insulting than this. The shrieking and shouting disturbed the ricebirds. They fluttered above the paddies and darkened the sky with their flapping wings.

The farmers heard the scream of a child, the sob of a mother, a wild shout, and an angry roar of troubled voices.

They did not stop to unyoke their buffaloes and let them have an afternoon rest. They did not check their fish nets and bring home the day's catch for dinner. They did not climb upon their buffaloes' backs and play their bamboo flutes as the animals plodded homeward. The startled men dropped their plowshares and ran.

By the time the rice farmers reached the village, the drop of honey, the lizard, the cat, the dog, and the two quarreling children were forgotten. Each man tried to defend his wife and soon found himself fighting his friends and brothers in a wild rush of fantastic fury.

The next day the villagers found themselves divided into two camps. Each side dug trenches, built barricades, and prepared for new battles. For twenty days and twenty nights they fought each other. Brothers killed brothers and fathers killed sons in a meaningless war.

The streets of Peaceful Village became littered with clutter. The houses were dirty and unswept. Weeds choked the

struggling rice plants. The water buffaloes' skin cracked because no one gave them their daily bath.

As the days passed it was evident that no one was really the victor, but no one was willing to give up. Finally, two men crept away and ran to the neighboring village for help.

"We must stop this foolish war. Please give us crossbows, poison darts, and food," they pleaded.

Their requests were ignored, but the shocking news of Peaceful Village at war was not. When the king heard about it, he immediately ordered soldiers to quiet the warring village. The villagers resented the interference and joined together in an effort to keep the king's soldiers away. After many days and many deaths the village became as still as the jungle at dawn. When all was quiet, the king's soldiers departed.

It is said the people in the village felt shame and sorrow.

"How foolish we were," the people said.

"This must never happen again," said the village elders.

"Let us learn from the experience and be calm forever more," said the village priests.

Neighbor bowed to neighbor and became friends again.

It is said, from that time onward the Thai people have been calm and have controlled their tempers. Their children are taught to be gentle and well mannered, but occasionally, like children everywhere, they are rash and act impulsively. Whenever this happens, the Thai mothers tell their children about the honey, the lizard, the cat, the dog, and the two quarreling children who started the war in Peaceful Village.

6. *The Gold Harvest*

Long ago in old Ayudhya there lived a man named Nai Hah Tong who dreamed of turning copper into gold. His wife, Nang Song Sai, had little faith in magic. She believed in the wealth of nature and richness of the earth. When her husband boasted, "Some day, we will be the richest people in Ayudhya," she listened patiently; however, when all their *tical* had been used for experiments, she decided something would have to be done about her husband's great expectation.

She said to her husband, "Nai Hah Tong, you have experimented with copper and a monkey's paw, copper and a lizard's tail. You have polished copper with the gold stripe of fur cut from the tiger's skin, but the copper did not turn into gold. Why don't you give up this dream and go to work like other men?"

Her husband said, "*Mai chai,* that is not right. With each experiment my magic has grown stronger."

"*Mai pen rai*, never mind, my husband, you must do what you must do," she answered.

The next day, however, she went home to see her father and asked him what to do about Nai Hah Tong's unreasonable search for gold.

Her wise old father did not seem disturbed. He said, "*Pai*, go now, and say nothing of this meeting. I have a plan to help your husband."

The next day Nai Hah Tong received an invitation to dine with his father-in-law. At *gingekow*, or meal time, Nai Hah Tong was there on the mat-covered floor beside the elderly gentleman.

The old man said, "My son, since you desire power and a long life, you sit facing east. I seek honor and dignity, so I shall sit facing west."

"*Chai*, yes, my father. I always follow the old belief. I never sit facing north when I eat, for I fear the bad luck such an action would cause, but sometimes, I eat facing south because I would like to have esteem and respect."

The old man smiled and nodded in agreement.

A servant interrupted the conversation by placing a large tray bearing bowls of white rice, hot chicken curry, roasted turtle eggs, vegetables, and *namprick*, a spicy sauce made from beetles and fish paste. Another tray held bowls of fresh water for washing, cloths for drying, and lime scent for perfuming the hands. The men ate from the same bowls, using only the fingers of their right hand. They did not speak very much while eating because the delicious food demanded their complete attention. The curry was spicy, yet sweet with the added milk of the coconut. The rice was fluffy and fresh from the top of the pot. The *namprick* bit the tongue, but it was good and made the mild coconut milk drink more tasty by contrast.

When the meal was over, Nai Hah Tong felt as content as a baby gibbon sitting upon his mother's lap.

"Ah, we are lucky for fish in the water and rice on the land," he said.

"*Chai,* my son, but there is more to life than good food. I have asked you to come to see me this evening because I need your help. Like you, my son, I have been looking for a way of turning copper into gold. Now, I know how to do it."

Nai Hah Tong drew in his breath and made a long, low whistling, sound. "Oh, it's too good to be true! I can't believe it!" he said.

"Listen carefully, Nai Hah Tong. I have everything I need for the miracle except one additional ingredient. Because I am an old man, I don't think I can work hard enough and long enough to get it."

"*Mai pen rai,* never mind, father. I will get whatever you need." Nai Hah Tong replied.

"That is not as easy as you might think, my son. I must have two kilos of soft fuzz gathered from the underside of the banana leaf, and the fuzz must be plucked carefully from your very own banana trees. Furthermore, I know the fuzz will not perform the miracle, unless it comes from a tree planted when magical words were spoken."

"I can say the magic words, and I can raise the banana

trees. I will collect the two kilos of banana fuzz for you." said Nai Hah Tong.

The old man smiled and said, "I know you can do this, my son. Because I have faith in you, I will loan you the money to buy the land you will need to raise banana trees."

The young man bowed low to the older. In the hearts of each of them there was a feeling of faith and trust.

Nai Hah Tong was determined to prepare his fields in a way which would be most pleasing to all the gods who might influence his crops. For this reason he went to his village *wat* and asked guidance from the priest who knew how to look at the gleaming stars and interpret the wisdom of the night sky. The priest's saffron robe glowed in the moonlight. His bare feet made no sound as he walked from the *wat* to the open court. The glittering stars seemed to light the sky as the fireflies light the darkness. The priest gazed at the stars as if they were the eyes of heaven.

Nai Hah Tong waited patiently for the priest. The only sound he heard was the lonely call of the gecko lizard hiding in a crack of the stucco wall of the *wat*. He counted the lizard's croaks—*nung, son, sam, see, ha, hok, jet.*

"Ah, it is a rare sign of good fortune. The gecko calls seven times, bringing me good luck."

The priest returned to his small, bare cell and opened a worn folding book. He said, "Since you were born in the Year of the Ox, you must begin your plowing on Wednesday, the tenth day of the fourth lunar month. Now, do not forget to begin when the sun is midway between the horizon and the highpoint of noon."

"*Chai, chai*, yes, yes. I shall do as you say."

The priest continued, "Before this auspicious hour you must build a shrine to the guardian spirit of the field, Phra Phum. Give him an offering of the best rice. Lay it flat on a shining green banana leaf and serve him graciously. At the north corner of your field, you must place three triangular white flags. As you mount them on bamboo poles, ask the blessing of the goddess who makes the banana tree fertile with the yellow fruit. Do not forget to praise the Earth Goddess and do remember to ask Phra Phum's blessing. Ask these gods to keep hungry locusts and nibbling worms far away from your fields."

"Is there anything else that I must do?" asked Nai Hah Tong.

"*Chai*, you will ask your village chieftain to guide your plow three times around the field. When this is done, again honor Phra Phum with the scent of incense and the beauty of flowers plucked by your own hands."

"All shall be done exactly as you desire," said Nai Hah Tong.

He followed the priest's suggestions and added one more touch of magic. With the planting of each banana tree he uttered the special secret words given to him by his father-in-law.

The gecko had predicted good luck, so Nai Hah Tong was not surprised when his banana trees grew tall, sturdy, and heavy with blossoms. Before very long he had thousands of firm yellow bananas and myriads of shiny leaves with a soft layer of fluffy fuzz on the underside.

Each morning Nai Hah Tong gave Phra Phum an offering of rice from the top of the pot. Then he carefully collected the soft fuzz from the underside of the banana leaves and stored it in a pottery jar. Each morning his wife, Nang Song Sai, gave Phra Phum flowers and incense. Then she collected the beautiful yellow bananas, took them to market, sold them, and placed her *tical* in a pottery jar.

After three lunar years had passed, Nai Hah Tong had half a kilo of banana fuzz. His wife had three pottery jars full of *tical*. Strangely, Nai Hah Tong was so intent upon collecting and storing the fuzz that he paid no attention to his wife's profitable labor.

One day Nang Song Sai's father came to ask if he would have to wait much longer for the two kilos of banana fuzz. When he saw the pottery jar partially full, he appeared worried. "I am an old man. If you don't get more land, more banana trees, and more banana fuzz, I shall not live to see copper turned into gold."

"*Mai pen rai,* never mind, father. I will borrow more money to buy more land. Then there shall be more banana trees and I can collect even more banana fuzz," said Nai Hah Tong.

Now Nai Hah Tong and his faithful wife worked for many years. The moons rose, waxed, and waned, days ran after days until finally the time arrived when each had accomplished a goal. Nang Song Sai had collected many jars full of *tical*. Nai Hah Tong had two jars full of banana fuzz. As you can imagine, it was an especially happy day. Nai Hah Tong shouted to his wife, "Run, run and bring your father here. Today he can test his magic. If all goes well, we shall see red copper glow until it is as gold as the sun of Siam."

When the old man arrived, Nai Hah Tong bowed very low before him and presented him with the treasured banana fuzz. The old man said: "Arise, my son. Today you will be a rich man."

Nai Hah Tong trembled nervously. Little rivers of perspiration ran down his face. His fingers shook like banana leaves in the wind. The old man, on the other hand, was not in a hurry. He turned to his daughter and calmly asked, "Have you made any money from the sale of bananas?"

"Oh, yes, *chai, chai,* my father," she said.

Nai Hah Tong thought his father-in-law must be out of his mind. When the copper was waiting to be turned into gold, why worry about the sale of a few bananas?

Nang Song Sai brought in a tray piled high with golden *tical* and placed it before her husband.

"Aha!" said her father. "Now, Nai Hah Tong, just look at all this money that has been made by following my directions. My son, I cannot turn copper into gold, but you and my daughter have harvested gold from the sale of your bananas. You cared for the young plants until they became trees producing delicious fruit. Is not that just as great a miracle as turning copper into gold?

Nai Hah Tong did not answer because he felt like a fool, but he was a very rich fool.

His clever wife knelt before him to show her love and respect. When she arose she said, "My husband, you are a master magician. With the help of the gods you cleared land. You cared for the banana trees with the same loving care we give our sons. You made the gods happy, and they rewarded you with the golden fruit of the banana tree."

"*Mai chai,* that is not right, my clever wife. Do not put a story under your arm and walk away with it. It is your father who is the master magician. He has made his honorable daughter and worthless son-in-law the richest people in Ayudhya."

Nai Hah Tong looked at the meaningless pile of banana fuzz mounted high on the table under the smiling face of his father-in-law. Right there and then, it is said, Nai Hah Tong mixed the banana fuzz with a little water and carefully molded a statue of the old man.

"What are you doing?" asked his wife.

"I am making a statue of your father. I hope our sons and our sons' sons will treasure it as a family heirloom. Each time they look upon it, they will be reminded of my foolishness and your father's wisdom."

It is said the statue can be seen in Ayudhya today. It is owned by a wealthy plantation owner who harvests gold, *chai* . . . gold bananas.

7. Brave Bear, Snake, and Crocodile Killer

Long ago in old Siam there lived a boastful rice farmer. Every day he said to his wife, "My dear, some day I will be a king."

His wife would smile and reply, "My husband, you are only a rice farmer with a small clearing of land near the forest. Put away your dreams and get to work."

The farmer remained silent after such a retort, but he never stopped dreaming of the day when he would ride the royal elephant and live in the royal palace.

One hot afternoon the farmer sat whittling wood while his wife planted rice seedlings in black earth. Suddenly she stood up straight and said, "Listen, I hear footsteps!"

"Shhh . . . it is coming closer!"

"What is it that growls so fiercely?"

"It is, it is, it is a–a–a bear," screamed the wife.

"Run, run for your life," shouted the farmer.

Without a thought for the safety of his wife, the farmer

rushed into the house and barred the door behind him. He fell to the floor trembling and crying with fear. When he managed to get to his feet, he peeked through a narrow crack in the door and saw his wife standing courageously with his whittling knife in her upraised hand. He closed his eyes, and then he heard a scream.

After a few moments of silence there was a scratching on the wooden door. The farmer ran into a far corner and huddled himself into a ball, with his head pressed against his knees. He could not believe his ears when he heard his wife's gentle voice say, "Open the door, my husband. There is no need to fear. I killed the bear with your knife."

The farmer yelled, "Go away! Have pity on me!"

He clenched his knees more tightly and said to himself in a soft whisper, "Its her spirit coming to haunt me."

The poor farmer could not escape the sound of his wife's voice, "Husband, stop your foolishness. The bear is dead! There is nothing to fear now. Come, we must finish our planting. Don't forget that a man who dreams of becoming a king, must tend to his fields."

The farmer hesitantly tiptoed across the bare wooden floor and peeked through the crack in the door. "Aha, it is you," he said as the color returned to his face.

As they walked back to the rice field the farmer said, "What will you say if someone asks, 'Who killed the bear?' "

"I will simply tell the truth. My husband, why do you ask such a question?"

The farmer coughed and then said, "Well, it seems to me that some people will not understand. Not very many women have killed bears, you know. Some people might be afraid of you, and some might believe you are a ghoul who killed the bear with a strange, magical power. My dear, to protect you from any possible unpleasantness, why don't we say that I killed the bear?"

At first the wife thought her husband's fears were foolish, but he convinced her that he should claim all honors from the bear slaying. The very next day the farmer went to the palace and told the king's guards about his brave deed. The king, who had always honored bear killers, said, "Very well done, my good man. You shall be rewarded."

He gave the farmer six rubies, two sapphires, and one lovely green emerald. Most important of all, he gave the farmer a new title. He bestowed upon him the glorious name, Hon Mee, which means Brave Bear Killer. Before very long every one in the small country spoke of him as the best bear hunter in all the land.

The king invited Hon Mee to live at the palace and for the first time in his life the rice farmer was happy. He loved the leisurely life of the palace and delighted in the luxury of royal treatment. He preferred the soft silks to the rough cottons he used to wear. The savory curries and spicy meats were far more delicious than rice and fish. All day and every day he smiled. His smiles won him many friends.

At least once in every lunar month he visited his wife who had remained at home to take care of the paddy. Now, when he said, "Some day I am going to be king," she listened to him.

Hon Mee's happiness did not last long, however. His

peace and rest was disturbed by a most unwelcome guest who had slithered onto the palace grounds. This frightful stranger was none other than Chong Ra-Ang, a giant cobra snake who had comfortably settled in the palace well.

When the king heard about Chong Ra-Ang's arrival, he summoned Hon Mee and said, "Brave Bear Killer, you must remove the cobra from our well." One never questions an order from the king. Hon Mee was trembling, but he managed to creep backward on his hands and knees until he was out of the king's sight.

Since the snake was resting quietly in a well, Hon Mee decided to call upon him.

Hon Mee bent over the well to get a better look at the loathsome creature, but unfortunately, he tripped against a stone, lost his balance, and tumbled directly into the well. He landed on top of Chong Ra-Ang. The massive cobra raised his sleepy head to get a better look at his unexpected visitor who, by this time, was splashing about in the water. Hon Mee did not know how to swim. He made a desperate effort to grab something, anything to keep from drowning. With a rapid stroke he swung around wildly and reached Chong Ra-Ang. He grabbed the snake just behind the head and squeezed so hard that he killed Chong Ra-Ang instantly. No one was more surprised than Hon Mee when he realized what had happened.

"Help! Help!" he called. A servant quickly lowered ropes to pull him and the dead snake out of the well.

The king smiled happily when Hon Mee gave him the dead Chong Ra-Ang. He said, "Hon Mee you have earned another reward." This time he gave Hon Mee twelve rubies, six sapphires, and two glittering white diamonds. Better than anything else, however, was the gift of a new title, Hon Mee Chong Ra-Ang, which means Brave Bear and Snake Killer.

Again Hon Mee Chong Ra-Ang settled down to a comfortable life in the palace. The servants pampered him. He grew plump and lazy, but never forgot his dream.

The next time he visited his wife she said, "Are you really going to be the king someday? Do tell me about your plans." He talked and talked until the crow of the rooster reminded him that it was time to return to the palace.

On the way back to the palace the little children from the villages gathered around Hon Mee Chong Ra-Ang and begged for stories of his brave deeds. He declined modestly and in doing so, won even more acclaim. The common people learned to love Hon Mee Chong Ra-Ang and cheered at the mention of his name.

Everything was going well for the former rice farmer, until one day the king sent for him to inform him about a horrible crocodile who lived in the river close to the village.

"This crocodile has acquired a great fondness for the taste of little boys and girls. He eats at least one for dinner every single day," explained the king. "Now, I want you to kill this ugly creature and bring me his dead body." Of course, the rice farmer could not refuse the king's request.

The next day the king gave Hon Mee Chong Ra-Ang a boat and the assistance of six brave men who were armed with rifles. As they departed, everyone in the palace cheered. The king shouted louder than all the rest, "Kill that crocodile!"

As the boat floated down the murky river, the rice farmer's knees were shaking, and as they crashed together, they made a strange noise like the sound of the noodle man's wooden blocks, telling his customers the noodles are ready. Every floating log frightened him. He groaned and moaned with terror. He was sick with fear.

Suddenly, Hon Mee Chong Ra-Ang heard his companions gasp. One pointed his oar toward the bank of the river. Hon Mee looked, closed his eyes, and looked again. There on the bank of the river, slithering down the mud embankment, was a giant crocodile.

The crocodile yawned. Hon Mee Chong Ra-Ang saw the mass of sharp teeth and fainted.

The six brave men calmly loaded, aimed, fired, and killed the crocodile with six blasts from their guns.

The gun shots brought Hon Mee Chong Ra-Ang back to consciousness. Now he was really sick. His head was covered with perspiration, and he felt a sharp pain in the middle of his stomach, but when he saw the crocodile still and lifeless, he immediately felt better. The six men shouted in six voices simultaneously, "The crocodile is dead!"

"Dead!" Hon Mee Chong Ra-Ang leaped to his feet and screamed at his men, "You have done a terrible thing! You all heard the king tell me to kill the crocodile. You have robbed me of my honors. When I tell the king what you did, he will tie you in bags and throw you in the river."

The six brave men hung their heads in shame. Hon Mee

Chang Ra-Ang turned his back on them and heard them chattering as noisily as the gibbons. Finally, their spokesman bowed to the farmer and asked permission to speak.

"We have a noble plan, Honorable One. We have decided to say that you killed the crocodile. We know you would have killed the crocodile if we had not done so. Now is there any real difference? If you agree to our plan, you may keep your honors, and we can keep our heads. Will you agree to our solution of this problem?"

Hon Mee Chong Ra-Ang agreed.

The six brave men tied a rope around the dead crocodile and the hunting party rowed back to the palace, dragging the dead reptile behind them. At the palace everyone was assembled, ready, and waiting to hear the exciting report of the great adventure. Hon Mee Chong Ra-Ang stood up in the little wobbly boat and simply stated, "The crocodile has lost his fondness for the taste of our boys and girls."

This brave deed merited a reward from the king. This time he gave the rice farmer twenty-four rubies, twelve sapphires, two glittering diamonds, and two lovely green emeralds. More important, however, was his new title. The king announced in a royal ceremony that from now on the rice farmer would be called Hon Mee Chong Ra-Ang Wang Chorake, which means Brave Bear, Snake, and Crocodile Killer. No one in the kingdom had a grander title.

Soon after this great event Hon Mee Chong Ra-Ang Wang Chorake visited his loyal wife who still took care of their small rice paddy. After he related his exciting adventure, she only asked, "When are you going to be king?"

Bear, Snake, Crocodile **63**

Now Hon Mee Chong Ra-Ang Wang Chorake intended to rest and relax. The bears remained in the forest, the snakes did not come near the palace well, and crocodiles did not eat the village boys and girls.

He closed his eyes and rested his head on a silken pillow while a servant fanned the air and another played sweet, regular rhythms on a clay drum covered with snake skin.

"Oh! now, this is the life!"

He was almost asleep when a messenger rushed into his room shouting, "Come quickly! The king needs you!"

Hon Mee raced down the corridors and fell to the floor before the royal presence of the king. At that moment the king declared a national emergency.

"The neighboring kingdom has raised a powerful army and is planning an attack upon our country. Hon Mee, I want you to be the Commander in Chief of all our men. We trust you will lead us to victory. If you succeed in driving this enemy from our borders, I will give you half of my kingdom."

"Your Highness, I will drive these demons from our country!" His answer was bold, but he felt weak.

That evening he crept stealthily through the forest to the camp of the enemy. Quietly, he climbed into a tree and stretched himself out on a slender limb where he could hear the enemy soldiers discussing their battle plans.

"Our only real problem is this great warrior, Hon Mee Chong Ra-Ang Wang Chorake. If we capture him, there would be no difficulty in defeating the entire army."

At just that moment the branch supporting Hon Mee began to snap and crackle. Both the branch and Hon Mee fell to the ground with a swooshing thud, right in the midst of the enemy. Without wasting a moment Hon Mee shouted, "I am Hon Mee Chong Ra-Ang Wang Chorake. Come and get me if you dare, but I warn you, I can fly into the air or dive into the earth. Furthermore, if anyone touches me I can turn him into stone."

The enemy soldiers dropped their crossbows and disappeared into the blackness of the jungle. Hon Mee picked up some of the weapons, whistled a gay tune, and walked back to the palace. He presented these trophies to the king and made his official report. "Your Highness, I tried to fight our enemies, but they ran away when I appeared in their camp. I don't think they will ever bother us again."

The king said, "Hon Mee, you are indeed a brave soldier, and you shall have half of my kingdom. When I die, you will be my successor."

The next year the king died and Hon Mee became the ruler of the land. His first official act was to send for his wife who had faithfully cared for their rice paddy during his long absence.

As she knelt before her lord and master she said, "My husband, I always knew you would become a king someday."

It is said that Hon Mee Chong Ra-Ang Wang Chorake ruled wisely and well, but his kingly duties occupied every moment of his time, and he never, ever went hunting again.

8. Phikool Thong

One day long ago a favorite wife of King Sanuraj gave birth to a beautiful daughter. When the royal astrologer was consulted regarding the baby's future, he said, "This child is as beautiful as the morning. She smiles as sweetly as a child of the gods but . . . but . . ."

"*Chai, chai,* yes, yes, go on," said the king impatiently.

"But . . . she will have a very strange habit. She will never be just like other children. However," he added very quickly, "do not despair. The child's unusual attribute will save her life one day."

The king replied, "She is a jewel of perfection. We shall guard her well. Perhaps, we can prevent this prophecy from coming true."

From that day onward the royal princess was observed carefully. It appeared she was a normal child with no bad habits. She did not suck her thumb. She did not bite her fingernails. She never pointed her toes at the *kwan,* the spirit, in one's head. She never forgot to bow properly with her hands clasped together. As a matter of fact, the child was delightful in every way until she began to speak, and then an unusual thing happened.

Each time the little girl uttered a word, a golden flower fell from her lips. When she sang and danced, the petals fluttered around her, and it looked as if she were in a lovely shower of flowers. When she sang herself to sleep, her mat was covered with golden petals. As she played with her cat and called him to her side, rose petals floated in the air. Because of this most unusual attribute, the king named his daughter Phikool Thong, which means Golden Flower.

In spite of her unusual habit it appeared as if the princess would lead a life of happiness. She was the king's favorite daughter, and often she was present when the king attended festivals. It was easy to recognize her because a little cloud of golden petals always floated about her.

On Kathin Day, when the rains were over and the first plowing of the rice fields began, Phikool Thong presented the priests with golden yellow robes. During the Songkran Festival, marking the beginning of the new year, Phikool Thong splashed lustral water on the hands of her parents as a mark of admiration and respect. At Loy Kathong time she joined her friends on the bank of the river and made a boat of banana leaves. She said a prayer to the Mother Goddess of the Sea. Then she placed a *tical,* incense, and a lighted candle in the little boat. According to ancient beliefs the little boat carried all her troubles to the sea.

For a long time it seemed as if the astrologer's predictions would not come true. Phikool Thong's life had not been in danger. But one day a most frightening thing happened when Phikool Thong was bathing in the river with her attendants. It was almost time to leave when she saw an ugly black vulture devouring the carcass of a dog. She screamed and her attendants screamed, too.

The princess was weak and almost faint from the sight and smell of the vulture, but she regained her composure and said calmly, "Come, come, let us leave quickly. The vulture's stench is making me ill. I hope I never see or smell another vulture as long as I live."

Phikool Thong returned to the palace, not realizing she had offended the ugly vulture. The bird she had encountered was no ordinary vulture, he was the King of the Vultures, a powerful creature who possessed the magic to turn himself into any shape and any form.

As the princess and her attendants ran to the palace he hovered above them and cast his black shadow upon them.

"You'll be sorry for insulting me," he said.

The very next day the vulture turned himself into a handsome young man and settled himself in a cottage with an old man and his wife. He gave them a chest full of jewels and said, the treasures in this box are yours, but first you must tell the king I wish to marry Phikool Thong."

The old people did as they were told.

The king was shocked to hear their strange request. He said, "Guards, find the daring young man who wishes to marry my daughter. Put him in a bag, fill it up with stones, tie it, and throw it in the river."

However, as soon as he said that, he changed his mind and decided to be more lenient. "Tell your young man to build me two bridges, one of pure gold and one of pure silver. The bridges must lead from your hut to the gates of the palace. If they are not completed in twenty-four hours, the young man will be put to death, but if the bridges are completed on time, Phikool Thong will be his bride."

The following morning everyone in the entire kingdom was startled to see two bridges leading from a simple hut to the gates of the king's palace. One bridge was made of pure gold and the other was made of pure silver.

There was nothing the king could do. A king must keep his word. The very next day, just as the king had promised, the Vulture King married the princess and took her away on a huge, black ship.

"Where are we going?" Golden Flower asked.

The Vulture King, who was still in the shape of a handsome prince, did not answer her.

Golden Flower trembled as she looked upon the strange, silent crew and smelled the unmistakable odor of vultures. She did not know that every crew member was a vulture in disguise, waiting to destroy her upon a signal from the Vulture King.

When the disguised Vulture King called the crew members into the captain's quarters, Phikool Thong seized the opportunity to say a prayer to the Mother Goddess of the Sea.

"Please, Mother Goddess, hear my plea. Send someone to rescue me."

Phikool Thong quickly took a golden flower from her lips and hid it in a silver locket. Then she tied the silver locket to a coconut shell and cast it into the ocean while saying, "May one, who is noble, chance to see and have the courage to rescue me."

Then Golden Flower heard a splashing sound against the side of the ship. It was the Sea Goddess saying, "Phikool Thong, look into the sky. Vultures swarm and vultures fly. Your prince, their king, leads the way. Hide yourself from light of day."

Phikool Thong dashed into the hold of the ship and swiftly crawled under a barrel. She huddled there without making a single noise while the vultures swarmed over the decks looking for her. Fortunately, they were not able to discover Phikool Thong's hiding place.

Later, when all was quiet, Phikool Thong emerged from under the barrel. The seas were calm beneath a clear blue sky. In the distance Golden Flower saw a graceful white ship. It seemed to follow a frothy white wave pointing toward her vessel. The princess shouted happily and hundreds of little golden flowers tumbled into the waves. They floated all around the ship, making a bright ring of gold.

On the approaching vessel stood King Pichai, the noble ruler of a mighty kingdom. He held Phikool Thong's silver locket in his hand and noticed the flower in the locket matched the flowers in the sea.

"Hurry men, hurry!" he called to his crew. "The princess is in danger."

As he spoke the sky darkened with a cloud of vultures

returning to find Phikool Thong. Luckily King Pichai was an excellent sailor, for in a few moments he was able to bring his ship close to Phikool Thong's ship. He managed to reach Phikool Thong's side just as the Vulture King swooped down and grasped her arm with his sharp claw. At that very instant the noble Pichai plunged his dagger into the Vulture King's heart, killing the evil bird instantly.

King Pichai and Phikool Thong fell in love the moment they met. The Mother Goddess of the Sea returned them safely to King Sanuraj's kingdom where they were happily married.

That year, at Loy Kathong time, King Pichai and his bride made a beautiful boat from banana leaves. They loaded it with the *tical*, the incense, the lighted candle, and then they added golden flowers from Phikool Thong's lovely lips. The little boat carried all their worries to the sea.

It is said King Pichai and Phikool Thong lived long and happy lives in a palace scented with the delicate fragrance of golden flowers.

9. Sri of Siam

Once long ago, when Thailand was Siam, the country was ruled by a most powerful man. So great was his influence that the mention of his name made men tremble, women hide, and children as still as pebbles along the roadside. As absolute ruler of all Siam, he held the power over life and death in the palm of his hand.

This great king lived a life of luxury. He sat upon a golden throne, slept upon a golden bed, and wore a tiered crown of gold high upon his royal head. His royal feet never touched the ground. He hardly ever walked. Kings in those days used a palanquin, a special kind of chair in which they sat proud and tall while servants carried them from one place to another. His food was served on plates of gold. His clothes were woven from golden thread. Understandably, the name of this king was "God Over My Head."

The king's servants and guards were tense beyond belief. Their eyes observed each motion and movement of his

73

hands, for even a gesture could mean a command. Their ears listened carefully for every word that he might utter. They responded even when he stuttered, whispered, or spoke in a roar. God Over My Head was a king no one could ignore.

There was a great fear in the heart of every man who lived at this time in old Siam. The farmers, the hunters, the astrologers, too, shared a fear with the men who trained elephants, the men who made bronze, the men who dug ditches and created *klong*. Everyone feared the king. He was, as his name implies, the god over their heads. No one dared to give advice to him, for the king's royal temper could very easily rise. But, in spite of the king, life was pleasant long ago. There were some folks who were most gay, but they were the ones who never heard the king say, "Put that man in a bag and throw him in the river."

Now, far away from the palace wall there lived a man who was not fearful at all. Unlike the king, the mention of his name made people smile and laughingly proclaim, "Sri is the wisest man in the land. Sri knows the mystery of sea and sand. Sri knows all there is to know. He is so smart, he hasn't any foe!" Sri Tanonchai was his name. The fame of his cleverness spread all over the land until he was known simply as Sri of Siam.

This man's memory was incredible. He knew everything by heart. People wore a path to his door bringing questions by the score. And strange as it may seem, he always knew the right answer.

"Sri, shall I be the father of a boy?" asked a proud young man one day.

"Ah, yes, you shall be the father of a–a–a baby. And if it is not a girl, most certainly it shall be a boy," said Sri with a smile.

Sri lived in a bamboo hut standing in the shade of a coconut tree on the bank of a lazy brown river. He sat on his haunches, as he had no chair. He slept on a mat on a floor that was bare. He ate rice and fish, and curry made from beef. More often than not his plate was a banana leaf. His clothes were made of coarse cotton thread. Straight black hair grew on his head. His eyes were sparkling black and bright, and as full of mischief and fun as there is heat in the noontime sun.

The fame of Sri reached every corner of the land. As luck would have it, the most royal ruler, God Over My Head, overheard his elephant trainer say, "If you don't know the answer, ask Sri. Puzzles, riddles, prophecy, past or future history, recipes, remedies, or cures for the cobra's bite, how to dance the *ramwong,* or how to fly a kite . . . Sri knows everything."

The king stood still and held his breath. "Why, this cannot be. That man speaks as if no one were as smart as Sri. I am the king of my country; never will it be said that a common man has more wit than God Over My Head."

He started out that very day on a mission of revenge. "I'll find Sri, and then we shall see who is the most clever!" he said to himself.

He rode his royal elephant in a rather haughty style, but

he dressed in a manner quite unlike a king. As a matter of fact, he looked like a king's elephant boy.

After a day, a night, and one more day, the king found his way to the door of the bamboo hut on the river's edge where Sri Tanonchai lived.

The king shouted with a royal roar, "Sri of Siam come here please, and bring your witty head."

Sri smiled a big broad grin instead of being cross. "*Sawaddi,* good day, good sir. Come and sit by my side, you appear to have had a very long ride. May I help you in some little way or did you come to pass the time of day?"

The king said, "Sri, I have heard of your fame, and I've come to put you to a test."

"Fine, fine," said Sri. "There is nothing I like better than a test to determine who thinks fastest and who thinks best."

"Sri," said the king, "are you as clever as people say?"

"Who knows?" said Sri.

"Not I," said the king. "That is why I am here. I came to find out, one way or another, if you are as clever as our king."

"But stranger, how can this be?" asked Sri. "The king has never sent for me. I've never seen the face or heard the voice of King God Over My Head."

"Sri, that problem is easy to solve, because I know the king most intimately and the only person as clever as he —is me! I can tell you with authority. I am his only equal."

"Your elephant has a noble look. No doubt you are one

of the king's best. Now, shall we match our wits in a simple contest?" asked Sri.

"*Chai*, yes," said the king. "This is what I propose."

"You may begin," said Sri. "I'll follow as I can. Perhaps, you have come prepared with some kind of plan?"

"Fine," said the king. "We shall match wits today. You must find a way to make me get into the river. You see, I've never liked even the thought of getting wet. Yet, a man who is clever could find a way of enticing me into the river."

Sri walked back and forth stroking his chin. There was a sparkle in his eye. He glanced at the river, at the king, and then with a sigh he said, "Good man, you are clever. Clever indeed! I would need magic to make you get in. I guess you win this part of the contest."

The king smiled victoriously as Sri continued talking.

"*Chai*, as much as I want to," he said stroking his chin, "I don't think I could ever make you jump in. But if you were in, and it were my task to make you get out—Oh! that would be the ultimate test of my cleverness."

For the king these words of victory were sweet. Without a pause, he made a leap from the bank to the muddy bottom of the river.

Sri began to laugh as he heard the king say, "Sri Tanonchai, you won't live another day if you can't get me out of the water right away. Prove how clever you are right now. Prove your wit to the King."

Sri's face was one big smile. "Your Highness, why don't you stay there and think for a while. For my part, you may

stay in the water forever if you wish. The river is full of
tasty fish, and I'll bring you a dish of rice now and then."

The king looked as if he were going to explode when Sri
said, "I won your challenge. There is no doubt. You asked
me to make you jump into the river, and there you are."

The king had no more to say. He had been outwitted in
every way. He climbed out of the river as lifeless as a broken
toy. He nodded to Sri, and said, "You are, indeed, a clever
boy!"

10. There Is No Such Thing as a Secret

The king of the country should have been the happiest man in the world. His country was at peace, the paddies produced large quantities of rice, and the royal astrologer predicted great good fortune. To make matters even better, a white elephant had been discovered at the beginning of the king's reign. With all this good fortune the king should have smiled all day long, but to tell the truth, and one should always tell the truth, the king was miserable. He never, ever smiled; his face was always long and sad. His eyes were dull and dreary.

Only one person in the kingdom knew why the king was sad. This man was the king's personal barber. The barber had been sworn to secrecy, and he kept the secret very well, so well, in fact, that no one even knew he shared the king's secret.

Each day the king looked more worried and depressed. The people in the court began to talk about their majesty's dejected expression. Some thought he had a grave illness, but the royal physician said, "He is as healthy as a water buffalo."

Others thought the country was going to suffer bankruptcy, but the royal treasurer said, "We have more wealth than the kingdom of China. Our royal treasury has chests full of jewels, our fields are full of rice, and our seas are full of fish."

Some said the king's many wives did not love him, but all the royal wives said, "We adore our noble king."

Three moons waxed and waned and the king's condition remained the same. Everyone knew he had a secret worry, but no one knew what it was.

One day the king's faithful barber became very ill. The king needed a haircut so a substitute barber was found. The new barber was as excited as a monkey with a handful of bananas. He had never served royalty and the thrill of actually cutting the king's hair was almost more than he could bear. He carefully washed his combs, polished his scissors, and wrapped them in a clean, white towel. Oh, it was a wonderful day! He skipped and sang all the way to the palace.

As soon as the barber arrived at the palace, the king, himself, swore the new barber to secrecy.

He said, "You must not tell anyone about anything you might discover today."

The substitute barber had one terrible fault. He could not keep a secret. Everything he did and knew gushed in a fountain of conversation. The barber was aware of his weakness, but the honor of cutting the king's hair was a rare privilege, so he took the vow and sincerely meant to keep it.

While he was cutting the king's hair, he became aware of something very strange. He said, "Your Majesty, now I know why you are sad. You should not let such a little thing trouble you."

"I cannot talk about it," said the king. "Barber, you must keep my secret."

The poor barber hurried home with an uncontrollable desire to tell somebody about the king's secret. He could not sleep. He could not eat. He refused to talk to anyone. The desire to share the secret grew like a huge swelling balloon inside him.

Finally, he could not bear the torture any longer. He hurried from his house and began looking for a lonely place where he could whisper the secret without having anyone hear him.

He rowed to the middle of the river, but to his dismay there were fishermen all around him. He walked away from the city and wandered on the paths between the rice paddies, but to his dismay there were farmers all around him. He went to the *wat*, but to his dismay, many others had come to the *wat*, and there were people all around him.

The secret was about to burst. The barber was desperate. He ran as fast as he could for as long as he could and then fell on his face in the tall wet grass. When he had rested for a few moments, he rose to his feet and discovered that he was alone in the king's royal forest. Right beside him was a hollow tree. "This is just the right kind of place. No one can hear me here," he said.

The barber wriggled into the hollow tree and then the secret burst. The barber shouted as loudly as he could. No person heard him, but every grain of wood in the tree absorbed the king's personal secret.

The barber wriggled out of the tree, hunched his shoulders, and sighed with relief. He skipped all the way home, feeling as light as a butterfly and as free as a breeze. It was, indeed, a wonderful day.

Not long after this the royal drum fell apart. It was very old and had had constant use. Each hour the royal servants had beat the drum to tell the passing of time. If there was anything the palace needed, it was a sturdy drum. The royal drum makers went into the forest and selected a tree· with fine wood. By coincidence, the very tree they selected was the barber's hollow tree, and every grain of wood in this tree had absorbed the king's personal secret.

The drum makers cut down the tree and had the royal elephant haul it into the courtyard. There they made a beautiful drum. They carved intricate designs on it and polished it all around. Then they selected the finest oxhide to cover the open end of the drum.

When the palace officials saw it, they said, "Let's invite everyone to see and hear this fine drum. Our king looks so glum. Perhaps, the new drum will cheer him."

The royal astrologers decided upon the proper day for the celebration. All the important people were invited to come. When the great day arrived, a huge crowd gathered in the courtyard. Everyone waited expectantly to hear the boom, boom of the new drum, but the new drum did not say, "Boom, boom, boom." Instead it bellowed forth the king's very own personal secret. The drum said, "The king has moles on his head. The king has moles on his head."

A little boy in the crowd began to giggle. Some of the other people felt like laughing, but they did not even smile. Everybody looked at the king. Now they knew why he had been so worried.

The king frowned and looked very cross. "Bring the substitute barber here," he shouted.

The barber's comb and scissors clicked in his pocket as he trembled in front of the king.

"Barber, did you tell my very own personal secret to the tree?"

The barber nodded and told the truth. One should always tell the truth, you know.

"Release him," said the king. "Let this be a lesson to all of you."

The crowd waited anxiously to hear their king explain.

He said, "Do not try to hide a blemish. No one person is perfect, and there is no such thing as a secret."

The great drum roared, "The king has moles on his head. The king has moles on his head."

The king nodded in agreement, and then he began to smile. His eyes began to sparkle, and his face was bright with happiness. The king was happy now because he had absolutely nothing to worry about. Everybody knew his secret.

ANIMAL AND BIRD STORIES

11. Why the Tiger Is Striped

Today the tigers in Thailand wear golden fur coats marked with bold, black stripes, but the tiger was not always dressed this way. Long, long ago the tiger's coat was not decorated with stripes. The tiger was a handsome beast who wore his golden coat like a royal robe. As he stalked along the jungle path in his beautiful coat, the gibbons, the monkeys, the parakeets, and the parrots all admired their handsome king. Without a doubt, the tiger was pleased with the style of his coat. As long as he could remember, no one had ever said anything uncomplimentary about it. If only he had not met the old man of the jungle, I do believe the tiger would still be wearing a coat of golden fur.

It all happened toward the end of the monsoon season one day when the rain fell so hard and so fast that it turned jungle paths into rivers. Each day it rained more, it seemed, and each day both man and beast became more concerned. No one could remember a season that had been as wet as this.

At the time of the great flood, an old man lived near the edge of the dark jungle. The old man's house was a simple bamboo hut placed on posts that were firmly settled in the ground. When the monsoon rains flooded the earth, he was high and dry. At night, when the jungle animals prowled and growled, the old man pulled up his long, jute rope ladder and slept soundly. Nothing bothered to come into his house, except the little *chingchok* lizards, of course, and since they ate the mosquitoes, he welcomed them.

All around the little hut was a bamboo fence. Within it there had been a vegetable patch, a mango tree, a betel palm, a clump of banana trees, and a pond. But now all one could see was a great pool of water and the tops of the trees. The pigs and chickens that had enjoyed the shade under the hut now lived in the house with their master. Each day the old man of the jungle had asked the guardian spirit of his little place to do something about the rain, so things could return to normal.

The guardian spirit must have heard him, because one day the rain stopped. The old man was very happy. He climbed down his rope ladder and began to work in his muddy yard. At lunchtime he paused to rest under his coconut tree. "Ah, there's a nice coconut up there, but I could never reach it without a long, strong coconut knife. Since it is such a beautiful day, I think I'll go into the jungle and look for rattan. I could trade a few bundles of rattan for a coconut knife."

He went on his way, stopping only in front of the guardian spirit's house to ask his blessing on the day's adventure.

A hot sun burned that day. There were no clouds in the bright blue sky. "I guess, the rains are almost over," the old man said.

As soon as the old man stepped into the jungle he felt the comfortable, refreshing coolness of shade. He smelt the sweet scent of a flowering vine that reached for the sun and cast a tangled shadow on his path. The pulse of a slight breeze seemed to rise and fall with the echoing call of a yellow jungle bird. The old man wandered deep into the center of the jungle before he paused to rest.

Suddenly, he felt a strong premonition of fear. A black shadow settled all around him. Before he could turn his head to see what was behind him, a huge golden paw knocked him over. A hot breath blew upon his neck. Then he felt sharp teeth piercing his shoulder. He screamed like a myna bird. The old man of the jungle had been caught by the golden tiger.

The old man thought fast and began to speak rapidly. "Oh, Phra Tiger, honorable tiger, put me down, put me down! Don't eat me!" he yelled.

The tiger tossed the old man over and held him securely under the weight of a heavy right front paw.

The tiger roared, "Speak quickly, old man. I'm hungry."

The old man cleverly replied, "Eat, eat me if you wish, but if you do, you will be dead by morning."

The tiger replied, "Old man, you wrap your tongue around your ears. Did you take a good look at yourself this morning? Did you dip up water with a coconut shell and look at your reflection?"

The old man laughed a little.

"That I did, Phra Tiger. That I did. I know if you eat me, you will be dead by morning!"

The tiger growled and shook his head. "Explain yourself," he roared.

"Phra Tiger, honorable tiger, if you free me, I could tie you to the top of a tree with heavy ropes of rattan."

"Now, why would you want to do a silly thing like that?" said the tiger.

"Haven't you heard? A great rain will flood our jungle this evening. All the village men are busy building rafts. I came to pick rattan so they could tie their logs together."

The hard gleam in the tiger's eye began to soften a little.

"Phra Tiger, you might fall from the top of a tree. Perhaps, I could build a raft for you and tie you to it. Then you would float safely on top of the floodwater instead of being drowned by it."

"Hummmrumgf," growled the tiger.

"Free me, Phra Tiger, if I don't start building your raft right now, it won't be finished in time."

"I'll free you," said the tiger, "but don't try to escape. I'll swallow you in one gulp if you do."

The old man did not try to get away. He quickly gathered sturdy rattan grass, tied logs together with it, and made a raft that was just big enough to hold the enormous tiger.

"Hurry, Phra Tiger," he called. "There isn't much time before the sky will darken and the rain clouds will burst."

The tiger lay on the raft and growled, "Tie me securely now. Don't do a careless job."

"*Chai, chai,* yes, yes, Phra Tiger," the old man said.

As the old man tied the last knot, securely binding the tiger to the raft, he smiled and commented, "You are a lucky tiger. No matter how much it rains, you will be safe."

The tiger purred like a contented house cat.

The old man placed both his hands together, bowed low before the captured tiger, and said politely, "*Sawaddi,* good day, Phra Tiger."

That night the sky darkened, but it did not rain. The next day it did not rain. The poor tiger was hungry and very sleepy. As each hour passed, he grew more angry. When two rising suns had burned the mist off two mornings, the tiger knew the old man had tricked him.

The tiger wriggled, squirmed, twisted, and turned. With each movement the slender rattan ropes cut more deeply into his beautiful golden coat. Finally, with a savage, desperate surge of energy he freed himself from the rattan ties that had bound him.

Oh, he was a ragged-looking tiger. His beautiful golden coat was ripped and slashed where the rattan had held him to the raft.

The tiger never recovered from the old man's trick. He repaired his coat, but he could not hide the mended black slashes. From that day on, the tiger of Thailand has worn a golden coat striped with the bold, black scars of his unfortunate meeting with the old man of the jungle.

As for the old man . . . he decided to get along without the long-handled coconut knife. "After all," he said, "there are more important things in life than coconuts."

12. The Tale of the Ricebirds

One late afternoon a mother ricebird sent the father ricebird to find food for their ricebirdlings. The father ricebird flew over a lovely blue pond and alighted upon a pink lotus. He knew he should not tarry, but he could not resist the temptation to taste the sweet lotus nectar. As he sipped and savored the sweet drink, the sun set and the shadows deepened into twilight. With the slow fall of darkness the lotus closed its petals, imprisoning the father ricebird in the fragrant darkness of a flower cell.

At dawn, when the lotus opened its petals to greet the sun, the father ricebird quickly hurried home to his family. He discovered his nest and his tree had been destroyed by fire. His children were nowhere to be seen, but he found his wife chirping sadly on the ground.

"Husband, while you tarried, a sudden forest fire burned our nest and all the little birdlings. Now I have no reason to live."

The husband protested, but his wife ignored him.

"I am going to hold my breath until I die," she said. "If I am reborn, I would like to be a human woman who escapes the pain of false love."

The father ricebird said, "I'll join you in death. If I am reborn, I wish to be a human man capable of winning my wife's true love."

The mother ricebird was reborn as a beautiful princess. The father ricebird was reborn as a handsome prince. The two never met, however, because the princess refused to speak to all men. In this way her dying wish had been fulfilled. She escaped the pain of false love by ignoring all her suitors.

One day the king said to his daughter, "You ignore every young prince who comes to court you. If you don't change your ways, I shall never be a grandfather. I have decided to give you in marriage to the first man who inspires you to speak."

The king's decision brought many princes to the palace. One gave the princess a necklace of sparkling jewels, but the glittering gems did not open her lips. Another prince brought the princess a beautiful speaking parrot, but the talking bird did not open her lips. A third prince presented the princess a *lakon,* or a troop of talented dancers, but the twirling performers were not able to open her lips.

One day the prince, who had been the father ricebird, came to the palace. He thought he could make the princess speak.

"Why are you so confident?" asked the king.

"I have a strange talent," said the prince.

"What can you do?" asked the king.

"I can throw my voice anywhere," said the prince.

"Indeed, he can," said the king's crown.

The king laughed and said, "If you can make my crown sound as if it speaks, there may be hope for you."

The king escorted the prince to the door of the princess's chamber and said, "If the princess has not spoken by daybreak, you must leave the palace and go on your way."

The prince placed the palms of his hands together and made a low *wai*, or bow, to the king.

He said, "When the princess speaks, I'll ring a bell. You'll hear its tinkle before you hear the rooster's crow."

"Good luck to you," said the king. He strolled down the corridor with a bounce in his stride.

The prince knew exactly what he wanted to do. Without wasting a moment, he threw his voice into the door and said, "Don't you know the princess will speak to no man? Why do you wait at her door?"

"I wait because the night is long and the princess needs to be amused. Door, may I tell you and the princess a story?"

"Please do," said the prince's voice, coming from the door.

The princess had never heard or seen a talking door. She huddled close to it trying to discover its secret.

"Listen carefully," said the prince. And then he told the following story.

"Once three men went to an astrologer who pre-dicted a most unusual event. Everything he foretold came to pass. The astrologer said the three men would soon see an enormous eagle carrying a beautiful maiden over a river. When the eagle soared above them, the first man, an archer, shot an arrow into the heart of the flying eagle, which dropped the girl into the river. The second man, a swimmer, dove into the water and rescued her, but his efforts to revive her were futile. The third man, however, had magical powers, and he brought the drowned maiden back to life.

"The astrologer, the archer, the swimmer, and the magician all claimed the girl as their own. Who do you think should have her?"

At the conclusion of the tale the prince peeped through the keyhole of the princess's chamber and saw her ear pressed against the opening.

"Door," said the prince, "who do you think should claim the girl?"

The door seemed to answer, "The swimmer, of course, for he rescued the maiden and brought her out of the water."

"Did you forget the archer? He rescued her from the eagle," said the prince.

"With more thought, I do believe the magician, the third man, should have her. After all, he did breathe life into the girl," responded the door.

Tale of Ricebirds **95**

All of a sudden the door opened and the princess stood in front of the prince. "Neither the archer, the swimmer, nor the magician should have her. She belongs to the astrologer who told of her coming."

"Sweet princess, you are absolutely right," said the prince. He rang the bell and awakened everyone in the palace. The king came bouncing down the hall, wearing a smile as broad as a crocodile's grin.

He proudly presented the princess to the prince. They were married the next day.

It has been said the prince never left the side of his beloved princess. Their lives were rich with joy and the happiness of the true love they had known long ago.

13. Why the Gibbon Says "Pua"

When the world was young and the stars were new, the gibbon did not swing from branch to branch on the trees in the jungles of Asia. In those distant days no one had ever heard of the gibbon, and, of course, no one had heard the gibbon say, *"Pua, pua, pua."*

Pua is the Thai word for husband. It is a strange word for a gibbon to say. However, each day as the sun slips from the sky, all the gibbons pucker their lips and utter sad, mournful cries, *"Pua, pua, pua."*

This story begins in that time of long ago when the gods shared their magic with mortal men. Of course, only the most holy and the most learned were allowed to use the magic of the gods. The chosen few were hermits who lived all alone in the middle of the wild jungle. They were protected by wild beasts that had been tamed by the hermits' cunning. Strong spirits gave further protection as the hermits meditated and communicated with the supernatural.

The hermits used to sit still for hours, with their legs crossed and their heads bowed in sacred meditation. They thought great thoughts and little thoughts on everything that existed. Ants, flies, snakes, fleas, flowers, eucalyptus leaves, bodhi trees . . . they thought about everything, from the meekest mouse to the most fierce tiger.

The hermits were virtuous men, and kindly, too. They tried to do good deeds and never harmed a living creature. All life was sacred to them, so they denied themselves meat and ate only fruits, berries, and blossoms of wild flowers. The king and everyone in the kingdom admired the hermits. They were the most kind, the most respected, and the most learned men in the entire land, and they were the only men who knew the secret magic of the gods.

Now it happened long ago that a grand and powerful king had a son named Chantakorop. When the boy reached manhood, his father decided to prepare him for his royal responsibilities. The king said to Chantakorop, "My son, you have seen the ways of men, but do you know the magic of the gods?"

"Father, only the hermits share the magic of the gods," the prince replied.

"I know, my son, and that is the reason I am going to send you to study with the wisest hermit in our land. To-morrow, you shall be guided to the hut of the hermit who lives in the northern part of our kingdom. He will try to teach you everything he knows. Be attentive and do as he directs. Those who disobey the hermit's directions bring misfortune to themselves and their loved ones. The royal astrologer has chosen your day of departure. He foresees only good things, if you do as you are told. Do you understand?" asked the king.

"*Chai,* I understand and I shall do as you say, father."

The next morning the royal elephants and an entourage of servants were ready to carry the prince to the jungle home of the hermit. As the boy departed, the royal astrologer tugged at his sleeve and said, "Do not disobey the hermit. If you do, your life will be in danger."

And so it came to pass that the young Prince Chantakorop moved into the isolated home of the hermit.

It is said, he would have been lonely if it had not been for the hermit's daughter, a beautiful, black-eyed maiden named Mora. When the prince was weary from a long day of study, Mora entertained him with her graceful dances. When he grew lonely for the gay life in the palace, she sang him songs of fellowship and cheer. When he needed nourishment, she brought him ripe bananas, the sweet sugared *phutsa,* and slices of delicious durian melon with its rich taste of mellow cheese.

The rainy season passed and the refreshing cool season began. "This is the time to gather roots and herbs from the jungle floor," said the hermit. He took the prince with him as he gathered twisted roots, green leaves, red berries, and brown bark from trees. All these things were used to make medicines, magic potions, and strange-tasting teas. With the coming of the dry season, the hermit concentrated on magic sayings, incantations, and the study of the stars. When the rain came, the hermit taught the prince to meditate, concentrate, and focus his thoughts on things as big as an elephant and as little as a poppy seed. It was believed the hermit taught the prince all the secrets of a lifetime.

The prince lived with the hermit for a whole year. During this time he studied diligently and did exactly as the hermit said. He never forgot the advice of his father and the warning of the royal astrologer.

When the time came for Chantakorop to return to the palace, the boy was sad and melancholy. He said to the hermit, "You and your daughter have been very kind to me. I know I must return to my home; however, I shall miss you both. My father will know of your goodness, and I trust he will reward you for your many virtues."

"Prince, I desire no rewards. My only goal has been to teach you the patience and the powers the gods have shared with mortal man. You shall take my wisdom and use it to rule well. Your success as a noble king shall be my great reward."

"*Sawaddi,* good-by," said the prince. He held his head high while the hermit bowed. A prince's head never bends lower than the head of a common man.

"*Sawaddi,*" said the hermit. "And now I have a gift for you. This clay urn contains your heart's desire. I trust you will treasure it forever. You may not open the urn until you can see the sun's rays upon the roof of your father's palace. If you should open it before that moment, an evil force more powerful than all my magic will bring you unhappiness and perhaps death."

The prince began the long journey with the urn in his

arms. With every step the urn grew more heavy, and the prince became more curious. "How can the hermit know my heart's desire?" he asked himself. "My heart yearns for Mora, his daughter. There is nothing I would rather have than Mora by my side."

Day after day the prince journeyed toward the palace. Daily the urn became heavier, and the prince more curious.

One morning the prince paused to rest. He held the clay urn up against the sunlight. It was as heavy as a stone, and he could not see through it. "Well," said the prince, "I shall not wait any longer."

He removed the lid from the urn. Then he drew in his breath and made a hissing noise. "This cannot be! How is it possible? Where did you come from?" The poor prince was so surprised and startled because Mora, the hermit's daughter, had magically appeared before him.

"My father knew that I was your heart's greatest desire," said the girl.

"You shall be my wife," said the prince.

"I shall love you always," said the girl.

Mora and the prince were married in the next village.

The prince was most anxious to present his bride to his father. He urged Mora to walk rapidly and hasten her steps. Each day they hoped to see the golden spires of the capital city, but each day ended in discouragement and despair.

"I think we are lost," said the prince.

"I don't think I can walk much farther," said Mora. She tried to walk rapidly, but fell in a faint.

"I shall give you my strength," said the prince. He slashed his thigh and used the blood from his own body to revive Mora.

No one knows for certain how they managed to survive their arduous journey, but it is known that one day they found their way to the edge of the jungle.

"Look!" said Mora. "I can see the sun gleaming on the roof of your father's palace!"

"Oooh, oooh," said the prince, groaning a little, for suddenly he remembered his parting with the hermit, and he was reminded of his broken vow.

At just that moment a bandit came along the road. When he saw the beautiful Mora, he decided to steal her from the prince.

The prince fought bravely. "You bandit," he shrieked. "Leave my Mora alone."

"I intend to steal her and keep her for my own," said the bandit.

The prince punched the bandit with his fist. Then he kicked him with his feet. The bandit sprang to the side and swung a powerful blow that sent the prince staggering to the ground.

The prince called to Mora, "Quickly, bring me my sword."

Mora held the sword behind her, waiting for an opportunity to give it to the prince.

The fighting made her weak for she had never seen such violence. The prince called, "Mora, quickly, give me my sword." The words revived her a little.

Mora managed to get to her feet. She held the sword forward, but unfortunately, the hilt was nearest to the bandit. The bandit did not waste a moment. He lunged forward, grabbed the sword, and killed the prince in an instant.

Mora bent over the body of her prince crying, *"Pua, pua, pua."*

The bandit took her by the hand and led her into the jungle. When they reached the darkness and the loneliness of the interior, the bandit became frightened. He deserted Mora and left her beneath a tree. She was dizzy, ill, and heart broken. All she could do was call, *"Pua, pua, pua,* husband, husband, husband."

As the sunset flamed the sky, the gods in heaven looked down on Mora and changed her into the gibbon. "Mortal men are not wise enough to use the magic of the gods," they said.

Today, men on earth no longer know the secret magic and powers of the gods. It is said the gods believe mortal men have grown evil, and until they become virtuous the divine secrets shall remain a mystery. The people of Thailand have never forgotten that time of long ago when hermits spoke with gods and shared their magic. To this day the gibbon's cry reminds them of the unfortunate result of a magical gift and a broken vow. In the gibbon's cry they hear the spirit of Mora grieving forever.

14. Manora, the Bird Woman

The romantic story of Prince Suthon and Princess Manora is one of the most popular of Thai folktales. It also has been presented in the form of a classical dance and in classical drama. The story is a Thai story, but it shows the influence of India and slightly resembles the ancient Jataka tale from India about a bird woman. Stories do change as they are told and retold. In the southern part of Thailand, Manora's name has been changed to Nora. This story, with a few slight variations, is also told in Malaya and in Indonesia and has become a part of their classical dance repertoire. The popularity of Manora reached a new height when the king of Thailand created a modern ballet based upon the adventures of Prince Suthon and Manora.

*   *   *

Long ago, in the oldest part of Siam, called Panchala Nakhon, there lived a handsome young man named Prince Suthon. He was the only child of King Athityawong and Queen Chanthathevi. The young prince was a remarkable young man, handsome, intelligent, and kind. It seemed as if he had mastered every grace and showed an aptitude for many skills, but in one sport, archery, he had exceptional ability. In the kingdoms to the east and west of Panchala Nakhon, Prince Suthon was called Good Arrow.

Good King Athityawong and Queen Chanthathevi were proud of their son and were determined to find him a wife who was as beautiful as the rose and as gentle as a doe. The king and queen observed many young ladies, but none of them showed promise of being a gracious and noble queen. One spoke with a harsh twang in her voice. Another lacked grace in her walk. The third was not clever enough, and the fourth was plain. The fifth could not sing sweetly. The sixth could not dance gracefully. The seventh lacked regal poise. When the eighth princess was rejected because she giggled too much, the entire kingdom became concerned.

One day, Boon, the most famous hunter in Panchala Nakhon, discovered the secret bathing pool used by King Tumerat's seven beautiful daughters. King Tumerat was a great king who ruled over the Bird People in the far north. It is said his daughters were the most beautiful young ladies in the world. They all wore soft-feathered wings that could be removed at will. Without the wings the Bird Maidens looked exactly like other girls.

When Boon saw the seven pairs of feathered wings lying on the grass, he quickly ran to the kind old serpent, the Naga of Champoo Chit, and borrowed his magic noose. Then he stealthily crept along the bank of the bathing pond and snared Manora, the youngest and fairest of all the Bird Maidens. Boon carried Manora to the palace and presented her to King Athityawong and Queen Chanthathevi.

"Princess Manora will make an ideal bride for our Prince

Suthon," said Boon. Boon's prediction was fulfilled, for Manora's natural loveliness and gentle charm captivated every member of the royal household.

Prince Suthon and Princess Manora fell in love and the entire kingdom rejoiced at the news of their wedding.

On the day they were wed the prince said, "Manora, I am the most fortunate man alive. My beautiful bride, I shall do everything I can to bring you happiness."

Manora answered, "Suthon, my only request is that you never leave my side. When you are near me, I am happy. When I am alone, I think of my father and my sisters and I become sad."

Unfortunately, Prince Suthon was forced to leave Manora soon after their wedding.

"I must help my father's soldiers defeat the enemies who attack at the northern boundary. Please understand," said the prince.

"I understand," said Manora.

The prince asked a trusted friend to take care of Manora. "Guard her well," he said, "she is the jewel of our kingdom, and the treasure of my life. Friend, do not neglect her. Watch her night and day, and as a reward for your service, I shall make you the Royal Court Counselor."

Suthon's friend promised and all would have gone well except for one thing, the old court counselor had overheard the conversation.

Late that night King Athityawong had a most strange dream. He called the old court counselor and said, "Last night, in my sleep, I saw my intestine unwind from my body. It rose like an enormous rope and wrapped itself around the entire kingdom of Panchala Nakhon. What does this mean?"

The jealous old man immediately saw a way to save his position. He rubbed his chin and looked very wise as he said, "Your Majesty, your dream is a sign that a great evil will soon fall upon you, your family, and the kingdom. So great is this evil that all may die in its grasp."

The king sat up very straight and whispered, "How can we prevent this evil from coming?"

"There is only one way to appease the gods, Your Majesty," said the court counselor.

"I'll do anything you say," murmured the king.

"You must make a blood sacrifice. You must sacrifice the Bird Woman."

"No," shouted the king, "Prince Suthon loves Manora more than anything in this world."

"Does she mean more to you and the prince than your own beloved queen and all your subjects?"

The king had no choice; yet, the horror of his decisions drove him into isolation. He placed guards at his door and ordered them to keep everyone away, including the queen.

The queen thought her husband had lost his mind. She spent each day trying to see him and then, when that failed, consoled Manora, "Don't worry, child," she said, "we shall find a way for you to escape."

"Good mother, you know Suthon would not want me to die. Please, bring me my wings," begged Manora.

The next day a crowd assembled to watch the blood

sacrifice. When the gates of the courtyard swung open, Manora was not tied to the stake. Her graceful wings were attached to her body. She was swaying as gently as a flower in the wind. Her arms moved slowly and her legs guided quick running steps. Suddenly, her wings stretched outward and as quietly as a swallow she flew over the palace and into the sky.

"May she reach her home safely," whispered the queen.

"I wish her well," said the king.

Manora flew immediately to the home of the wise old hermit who lived in the clearing near her bathing pond. She paused just long enough to say, "Wise One, if my husband comes to find me, please give him my ring of red rubies."

"Bird Maiden, you know the prince will seek to the ends of the earth for you. I shall give him your ring and my blessing."

Manora's eyes filled with tears as she said, "What you say is true. Please, try to protect him from harm. Will you teach him the prayers which will protect him from evil?"

"I will do that and more, Manora. I shall teach him the language of the birds and animals, and I shall give him some powerful magic."

Manora gently fluttered her wings and flew into the sky, heading in the direction of Mount Krailot where her father and six sisters were waiting to welcome her home again.

As soon as Prince Suthon discovered what had happened,

he set out to seek his wife. For many days he traveled into areas where no one had gone before. Wherever he went he asked, "Can you direct me to the land of the Bird People?" But always the answer was the same until the day he discovered the wise hermit of the north country.

"Yes, I can direct you to the land of the Bird People. The way is perilous, but if you know the secret prayers, and carry my magic lotion, I think you will be able to arrive there safely. For added protection I shall give you my pet monkey. Never put a berry or a jungle fruit in your mouth unless the monkey eats it first," said the hermit.

"If you do all this, I shall be eternally grateful," said the prince.

The hermit gave Prince Suthon Manora's ring of red rubies, taught him special prayers, the language of beasts and birds, and directed him northward. For seven years and seven months Suthon traveled through jungles, forests, thorny fields, and over the highest mountains. Then he met a monstrous creature called the Yak.

The Yak stood seven times taller than the tallest man. His breath was a flame of blue fire. Smoke sifted through his nostrils and rose into the sky. Prince Suthon said the secret prayers, and the fierce Yak knelt down before him.

The next obstacle was a river of blazing, dancing red flames. The prince said the secret prayers and immediately a huge boa constrictor appeared. He stepped upon its back and safely rode over the river of fire to the opposite bank.

The prince had scarcely taken a dozen steps when he discovered his path was blocked by an enormous tree unlike any he had ever seen before. The thick jungle growth prevented him from going around it. The strong, sturdy roots prevented him from digging under it. With no alternative, the prince climbed the tree, but fell asleep in the branches.

The next morning he was awakened by the chirping of two great birds. They were larger than tigers and wore glittering feathers of sparkling gold and gleaming feathers of shining silver. Prince Suthon listened carefully, and to his great surprise, he discovered that he was able to understand the birds.

The first giant bird said, "If we go to Mount Krailot tomorrow, we shall have a feast."

"Oh yes, I heard King Tumerat was having a celebration in honor of his youngest daughter. By all means, we should go, but first we must rest. Mount Krailot is far to the north," the second bird replied.

Prince Suthon unleashed his little monkey and set him free. Then he climbed on the back of one of the huge gold and silver birds and nestled under the metallic feathers.

Early the next morning the great birds stretched their wings and flew directly to the lotus pond in King Tumerat's garden.

Prince Suthon arrived just in time to see a party of bird hand maidens carrying golden pitchers to the pond.

"Our Princess Manora cries all day, no matter what we do. She yearns for her prince who is far away beyond the mountain blue," sang one little servant.

"Good maiden, are you carrying your golden pitcher to Princess Manora's chamber?"

"Indeed, I am," said the little girl.

"It is a heavy burden for one so small," said the prince. "Here, let me carry it for you."

The prince slipped off his ring of red rubies and dropped it into the golden pitcher.

When the hand maiden splashed her pitcher of water over Manora, the ring of red rubies clinked before her.

"Tell me quickly," shouted Manora, "have you seen a strange man in our garden?"

"Yes, My Princess, he helped me carry the golden urn full of water."

Manora grabbed her servant's hands and danced merrily around the room.

"Quickly, take perfumes, jewels, and silken clothes to him. He is my husband, and he must be dressed properly before he meets my father."

An hour later Prince Suthon was presented to Manora's father, the great King Tumerat.

"Prince Suthon, we Bird People are impressed with your devotion to Manora; however, before you may claim her as your own, you must prove yourself worthy."

"Your Highness, I have traveled for seven years, seven months, and seven days looking for Manora. Now that I have found her, I shall do anything you request in order to gain your blessing on our marriage," said the prince.

"Your first test is a test of strength. Can you lift the solid stone bench in my garden?"

Prince Suthon calmy walked to the bench, knelt before it and prayed to the gods for strength. The next moment he grasped the stone bench and raised it above his head. The gasp of those present was like a swish of wind in the tree-tops.

"Well done," said the king. "Now, since you wish to take Manora from her homeland, you must prove that she is the only maiden you desire. Can you select her from a group of seven young ladies?"

"I would know Manora anywhere," said the prince.

But he wished he had not spoken so quickly because the next instant seven identical Manoras danced in front of him. The prince prayed to the gods for help and in response a golden butterfly appeared. It flew three times around the head of the girl in the center. Prince Suthon took her hand, led her to the king, and said, "This is my Manora." The king smiled with approval.

"Only one task remains, Prince Suthon. You must shoot an arrow through seven palm boards, seven figwood boards, seven plates of copper, seven plates of iron, and through seven bullock carts filled with sand. If you can do this difficult task, Manora shall be yours forever."

The prince did not pause for a moment. After all, his name had come to mean Good Arrow. With one quick, sure stroke he placed his sharpest arrow in his crossbow and let it fly. Like a stroke of lightning the arrow pierced through the palm boards, figwood boards, copper plates, iron plates, and sand-laden bullock carts. It is said that even then the arrow did not waver as it soared straight into the open sky and disappeared from view.

The king watched the arrow fade into the distance and

said, "Prince Suthon, you may take Princess Manora to your homeland."

From that eventful day until the end of their lives, Princess Manora and Prince Suthon lived happily ever after in the prosperous kingdom of Panchala Nakhon.

15. Why the Crow Is Black

Have you ever seen a peacock prance in a beautiful meadow of emerald green grass? It is delightful to watch his long train of feathers ripple over the lawn like a flowing rainbow. The brilliant crest on his head sparkles like a king's crown and the bright-colored feathers on his breast are worn as a necklace of precious jewels. After a few struts, the peacock pauses and spreads his magnificent tail, revealing circled patterns in an elaborate fabric of soft feathers. He holds his head high, and if he could speak, he would say, "I am the most beautiful creature in the world. You may admire my loveliness."

The crow, unlike the peacock, is an unattractive bird. His voice caws in a harsh, ugly twang. His black feathers are often frayed, worn, and smudged with dirt and dust. He does not clean or preen his feathers, and no one enjoys watching him strut.

In the long distant past, the peacock and the crow were

birds unlike any that exist today. The peacock was not a proud, prancing bird of beauty. The crow was not black. Both birds were white, white as clouds, and neither peacock nor crow ever complained about the unexciting color of their feathers. The appearance of the birds was different, but their personalities were just the same as they are today.

Strangely enough, the peacock and the crow were the best of friends. They played together on the sands near the sea. They cooed songs to each other and told stories for their mutual pleasure.

All the animals of the world knew the crow and the peacock were friends, but they could not understand why such a close bond existed between them. They said to one another, "The crow is white and the peacock is white, but in every other way the two animals are different."

Every animal knew the crow was a bad housekeeper. His nest was always messy. The crow had another bad habit, he wore dirty feathers. He never took time to bathe, and as a result, he was frequently seen with smudges and soiled spots all over him. The crow's appearance was deplorable, and he was even less concerned about what he ate. If he saw a morsel of food in a pile of garbage, he swooped down and gobbled it up. The crow ate carrion, rotting fruits, and whatever was available.

The peacock, however, was neat and clean. He was proud of his beautiful white feathers and bathed several times a day in order to keep them white. His nest was always in order for he was an excellent housekeeper. The peacock often scolded his friend about his diet and his way of living.

"Don't eat the spoiled food," he insisted. "The clean grains and fresh fruits will keep you well and strong. Drink the fresh spring water, Friend Crow. It is so much better for you."

One morning, when the peacock had finished bathing, the crow came by to chat. He was covered with mud from his beak to the tip of his tail. The peacock's feathers were so clean that they sparkled in the sunlight. The crow said, "Have you spent all morning washing yourself?"

"Indeed, I have done just that," said the peacock. "It appears as if you need a good scrubbing, Mr. Crow. Would you like me to wash your back?"

The crow consented reluctantly.

As the peacock bathed the crow, he said, "Oh! how I wish we had colorful feathers. Reds, blues, and golden hues would thrill the eye and bring delight to everyone who saw us."

"What difference does it make?" said the crow.

"Friend Crow, we could be the most beautiful birds in the world. If I painted your feathers and you painted mine, we could have coats that would glow and sparkle and shine," said the peacock.

"All right," said the crow, "I'll do as you wish. Shall I paint you first?"

"Yes, but you must do exactly as I say," said the peacock.

The peacock carefully directed the crow's strokes. Hours passed and the peacock became more lovely with each touch of the crow's brush. When the crow wanted to stop the peacock said, "No, no, you must go on."

Finally, the peacock's feathers were completely covered with a beautiful array of colors, and the peacock was excited with the result. He strutted around spreading his train and rippling his feathers in the sunshine.

"How wonderful! Now Friend Crow, it is my turn to paint you," he said.

The peacock cleaned the brushes and carefully mixed his paints. At the moment he was ready to begin, the crow saw a dead dog floating down the river. The sight of a possible dinner floating by made him most impatient. "Peacock," he said, "quickly, paint me as fast as you can. Use only one color now and do paint rapidly!"

Please, be patient, Mr. Crow. I wish to make your feathers as lovely as my own," said the peacock.

The crow cawed in desperation, "Just throw the black paint on me! I am hungry, and I cannot wait another moment."

The peacock did as the crow demanded. He hurled the bucket of black paint, and with one enormous swoosh the crow became black. As he flew toward the river, his feathers dripped black spots of paint behind him.

From that day to this the peacock has had beautifully colored feathers, and the crow's feathers have remained black.

The moral of this story is beauty comes to those who pursue it.

RELIGIOUS STORIES

16. The Emerald Buddha

Five hundred years after Buddha's death there lived a wise and holy man named Nagasen. He was so devoted and so dedicated to the teachings of Buddha that he became a monk in a temple called Asokarem in the city of Padalibutra, India.

When Nagasen knelt reverently in prayer, his being filled with love for Buddha. When he studied the holy scriptures, his mind embraced the words and they became his principles, his path, and his purpose. For many years Nagasen studied the teachings of Buddha, and with each passing year his love unfolded like the petals of a rose. Now his love for Buddha had reached full blossom. There was a noticeable change in Nagasen. His eyes sparkled with confidence, and his words aroused the people who had forgotten Buddha's creed.

The greatest change in Nagasen occurred within his heart. A sadness settled there. A sadness which was destined to cause the great god, Indra, both alarm and concern.

One day Indra sent for his friend Vishnu and said to him, "I know all thoughts of men; I know all actions of men; I know what came before, and I know what is destined to be. Now I know that Nagasen's heart is heavy, and he struggles to share his love for Buddha. Vishnu, I ask you to come with me to the temple of Asokarem. We shall speak with Nagasen. We shall lighten his heavy heart, and help him find a way to share his bountiful love."

Indra and Vishnu waited for Nagasen in the Asokarem temple garden. It was springtime and jasmine scented the air. Peacocks strolled proudly by the bushes which were heavy with awakening buds. From the temple came Nagasen with a face glowing with love for all creatures. When he saw Indra and Vishnu, he fell to his knees and bowed low.

"Arise, Nagasen, be not afraid. We have come to lighten your heavy heart. Speak now of your problem."

"Oh! Indra, you know this love of Buddha is a treasure to be shared. If we had an image of him, a likeness of his features, everyone could worship him and show their reverence. The image must be made to last forever, but I do not know how to make the image or where to find a jewel precious enough for the privilege of bearing Buddha's likeness."

"Your problem shall become my problem, Nagasen," said the great Indra. "Go now, Nagasen, and worry no more. I, Indra, will help you."

Nagasen returned to his temple, and Indra said to

Vishnu, "Go now and get the most precious of all stones from the Mountain of Velu."

Vishnu stood as still as a stone. His eyes were downcast. Beads of perspiration like drops of dew dotted his forehead.

"Vishnu," said Indra, "what troubles you?"

Vishnu was silent and still. Again the great Indra spoke, and this time his voice was a roar of anger and impatience.

"Vishnu, why do you not answer me?"

Vishnu fell to his knees and sobbed as a child cries when he is afraid, and he is forced to go alone into the dark.

"Oh, Indra, you are my master, and I would willingly go anywhere for you, except to the Mountain of Velu. The precious stone Nagasen seeks is guarded by demons who can turn even a god into mist. The fires from their breath can scorch the earth for miles around. The arrows from their bows turn to hissing snakes. There are giants who stand guard with the demons. Their heads tower above the trees. With a snap of their fingers they crumble a man like a wafer, and even a god isn't safe in their grasp."

The perspiration ran down Vishu's face. His lips trembled.

Indra spoke, "Be not afraid, Vishnu. We will go to the Mountain of Velu together."

Like giant creatures of the sky, they stretched their arms and flew more rapidly than eagles to the Mountain of Velu.

The demons and the giants guarded this mountain as carefully as the kings of Siam guarded their white elephants.

Although the demon's appearance was horrifying, Indra showed no fear. Vishnu walked cautiously behind him as they slowly approached the demons and the giants. When they were close enough to stand in the shade of the giants, he said, "I am Indra."

So great a god was he, that even the giants and the demons bowed before him.

"Indra, we are honored by your presence. How may we serve you?" the giants asked.

Indra said, "I have just one request. Give me the precious stone that is guarded here."

The giants moaned, and it sounded like thunder. The demons turned themselves into a whirling wind. Vishnu shook like a lone blade of grass in the monsoon wind, but Indra stood calmly waiting for a reply.

"Why do you want it?" a demon asked.

"I wish to give the stone to the Buddhist priest, Nagasen. He will use it to make an image of Lord Buddha. The image will inspire reverence for Buddha and bring those who doubt a reminder of Buddha's goodness," said Indra.

The moans turned to whispers and the whirling demons stopped spinning.

A great giant said, "The stones we guard belong to Isvara, a king who dwells on the highest peak of the Himalaya Mountains. King Isvara has saved three thousand beautiful gems. We guard his treasure for him. We also guard another jewel more lovely than any in the world. It is a rare block of precious jasper jade."

"Please, tell us what it looks like," said Vishnu.

"Have you ever seen the stars beneath a soft green mist? Have you ever seen the moon behind a spring green haze?

Have you ever seen the sun's rays penetrate a billowing cloud? If you have, then you know what the stone looks like," said the giant.

"Is it possible for one gem to possess such mysterious beauty?" asked Indra.

"When I see your gem, I shall believe your words," said Vishnu.

The demons and the giants said in unison, "You will believe, and you will see with your own eyes the most beautiful of all stones."

"Please, give this precious gem to Nagasen," urged Indra.

The giants and the demons said, "We shall give it with our love to honor Lord Buddha."

A demon whirled like a cloud of dust and vanished into the mountainside. When he returned, he held the precious gem draped in shimmering blue silk. He slowly slid the silk from the block of jade, and the stone seemed to radiate a soft green glow.

The demon gave the stone to Indra and said, "Give this to Nagasen with our wish that it shall please him."

The gods carried the jewel to the garden where Nagasen strolled each day. They placed it on his favorite bench and waited for him to find it. At dusk Nagasen appeared and sat on the bench to observe the setting sun. Vishnu removed the silken covering and the stone rivaled the beauty of the sun. Tears of joy flowed from Nagasen's eyes. So great was his joy that his lips could not form words to speak of his happiness.

Vishnu and Indra did not need words for they knew of the happiness in Nagasen's heart.

Indra returned to his abode in the sky, but Vishnu remained in the garden. He transformed himself into the shape of a mortal man and stood beside Nagasen's enormous gem.

"Nagasen, will you allow a poor stonecutter the pleasure of holding your precious stone?" he asked.

"Old man, you may put your chisel to work. Take the block of jade and carve from it a likeness of Buddha," said Nagasen.

Vishnu did as he was directed. When he returned the jewel to Nagasen, it had been transformed into the gleaming Emerald Buddha. All the colors of the rainbow flowed from the stone in a soft green haze of light. Nagasen was delighted, and both Indra and Vishnu knew of his special joy.

The Emerald Buddha was placed in a beautiful temple, a *wat* with a roof of gold and a floor of marble. It fulfilled Nagasen's great dream of sharing his love for Buddha. So great was the statue's beauty that giants, demons, gods, and myriads of men came from ten directions to admire it. From that time long ago until the present, the Emerald Buddha has inspired all who see it, to live the life of noble virtue recommended by Lord Buddha and encouraged by his loyal servant Nagasen.

17. The Footprint of Buddha

Many years ago there lived a group of young Buddhists who were new *bhikku,* or monks, in the *sangha,* the Buddhist priesthood. They decided to make a religious pilgrimage to the footprint of Buddha on the crest of Adam's Mountain in Ceylon. The great father of their *wat* said to these younger brothers of the *sangha:* "The journey to Ceylon is dangerous. Snakes, crocodiles, and tigers will cross your path."

"We are not afraid. We believe in Buddha's goodness," they answered. "Look, our legs are as sturdy as the branches on the teak. Our faith and our feet will carry us through the jungles to the true footprint of Buddha."

Their departure was a beautiful sight to see. The priests' golden robes gleamed in the sunlight and fluttered like banners in the tropical breeze. The very grass they stepped upon seemed to glitter green with the touch of their bare feet. The elder priests beat the gongs in the *wat* and the metallic booms resounded with a pulsing rhythm, announcing to everyone that the young brothers of the priesthood were beginning a holy journey.

Like all Buddhist priests these men desired to become pure in heart and pure in deed. The Patimokkha, an ancient collection of religious laws, directed their behavior. They were permitted to own five items, a bowl, the robes on their backs, a razor, an umbrella, and a square of cotton cloth. The razor shaved their heads. The metal bowl with a shining brass rim held the rice they ate. The cotton cloth strained insects from their drinking water and their tea, a necessary precaution, because the Patimokkha forbade them to take the life of any creature, and they did not even want to kill an insect by swallowing it.

Each morning the priests awakened before dawn and walked from village to village. The farmers gave them food most willingly, for they gained religious merit by placing a serving of rice in the priests' bowls. As they offered a helping, they said, "*Khop khun krap,* thank you, for the privilege of serving you."

Day ran after day and finally the priests reached their destination, the shrine of the sacred footprint in Ceylon. The Ceylonese priests were surprised to see their brothers from Siam. "Were you not afraid to travel all alone in the jungle?" they asked.

"We were not afraid. We believed in Buddha's goodness," they answered.

The priests from Siam placed red, white, and yellow flowers before the shrine of the footprint. Near the flowers they lighted sticks of incense, making the air sweet and heavy with delicate fragrance. As they said prayers of thankfulness, they bowed low and kissed the sacred earth where Buddha had once stood.

When they arose the Ceylonese priests said, "Why have you come here to worship our footprint of Buddha? Our ancient scriptures tell us there is a footprint of Buddha located upon the Golden Hill in your country."

The Siamese priests doubted this. "It cannot be true."

The Ceylonese priests said, "Our ancient scriptures prove our words. Look, the holy writing on the dried palm leaves tells of a footprint of Buddha on the Golden Hill in Siam."

The Siamese priests hurried home so fast that at times their golden robes seemed like fluttering wings of tawny birds floating through the jungle. They told King Song Dharm about their miraculous discovery. The king was more happy than a hunter with a dead tiger at his feet. He immediately began the search for the footprint of Buddha. The king's men looked on Golden Hill and on all the mountains and in every valley, but they could not find the footprint.

Day ran after day. The grasses grew tall in the tropical sun. The trees stretched their limbs to greater heights. The river flowed into an ebbing sea, and the ancient country of Siam grew older with each setting of the red-tinted sun.

The young priests who had made the long journey to Ceylon were now the great fathers of their *wat*. Their brown bodies were as wrinkled as the withering palm leaves which told of their country's lost treasure. Their voices were a faint whisper now, but they never stopped talking about the footprint.

"It is lost like a ruby in a basket of rice. We must sift each grain to find our country's lost treasure."

Some people doubted and accused the priests of hearing a story, tucking it under their arm and walking away with it, which is a Siamese way of saying the story is not true. Although many doubted, the priests said every day, "We will find the footprint. Believe in Buddha's goodness."

Their faith was rewarded, for one day a farmer ran into their *wat* shouting like a dancer at a rice festival, "Boon found it! Boon found the footprint of Buddha. Come to Saraburi. Hurry, he is going to tell us how it happened!"

The old priests hobbled as fast as their bare feet and aged limbs could carry them. When they arrived in Saraburi, they found the hunter, Boon, in the market square with a crowd of curious people gathered around him. As Boon began to speak, the crowd hushed. The old priests leaned forward to hear each word.

Boon said, "I was hunting a small spotted deer with my crossbow on Golden Hill. The deer paused for a moment, I aimed, and let my bamboo arrow fly. It pierced the flesh, and blood ran from the wound like tears of death. The deer didn't fall to the ground. He limped into a thicket of tall green grass. I ran after him, but before I could catch up with him, he bounded from the grass with the vitality of a yearling. What is more surprising, my arrow was not in his side, and his wound was gone.

"I followed the spots of red upon the earth. They led me

to a pool of clear water. It was like a sapphire glittering in the sun. All around it the moss curled rich and green. The deer's footprints stopped by the little pool. I thought the deer must have stopped to drink so I, too, paused to drink some of the water. One swallow of the water cooled my hot body and made me feel as clean as a white lotus.

"Suddenly, I felt very well. All my life I have had red sores itching my arms, but then the sores disappeared, and I felt as strong as an elephant pulling teak logs.

"I was dizzy with delight. I splashed in the pool until all the water had spilled upon the earth. There, at the bottom, I found the imprint of a human foot. It is the footprint of our Lord Buddha."

The priests' hearts beat faster with every word Boon uttered. A light of contentment gleamed in their eyes. It is said they climbed the Golden Hill with a determined stride like the young priests of old who had climbed Adam's Mountain in Ceylon.

They fell silently upon their knees before the sacred footprint. Their lips uttered the prayers of thankfulness that overflowed from their hearts.

"*Khop khun krap*, thank you, Lord Buddha. We believe in your goodness," they said.

People still speak of the great surge of joy that filled the hearts of everyone in old Siam on that wonderful day long ago. From that day to this the footprint of Buddha has been a sacred treasure. It reminds everyone of Buddha's faith in the goodness of man.

18. Phya Paan and the Golden Chedi

One of the most sacred memorials in Thailand is the Golden Chedi of Pra Pathom. Its orange-tiled stupa towers high above the small town of Nakhon Pathom, located thirty-five miles west of Bangkok. This ancient Buddhist monument is the oldest and largest structure in Thailand; yet, for many hundreds of years it was hidden by jungle growth. Thailand's famous King Mongkut discovered the ruins of the Golden Chedi during his wanderings when he was a Buddhist priest. Later, when he became king in 1821, he began the restoration of the monument. His successor, King Chulalongkorn, completed the renovation. Today the original stupa cannot be seen because it is encased in a larger one which is covered with brilliant orange-gold tiles, some of which were laid by King Mongkut himself.

The inhabitants of Nakhon Pathom tell a story about how the Golden Chedi came to be built. It is the legend of Prince Phya Paan whose tragic life fulfilled the predictions of the court astrologers.

*　　*　　*

Long before your grandmother's grandmother was born there was a mighty ruler in the old Siamese kingdom of Kanburi. His people called him King Phya Kong.

One day his queen gave birth to a son. The new prince was a handsome child and his father found great joy in him

133

until the court astrologers came to the palace and made their dark prophesy about the boy's future.

"Will our son be a famous ruler?" asked the king.

"*Chai*, oh yes. For generations your son's name will ring on the lips of every person in Kanburi," said one astrologer.

"Will he be a kind and good man?" asked the queen.

"He will bring suffering and sorrow to those who love him most," said another astrologer.

"What do you mean?" demanded the king.

The oldest and the wisest of the court astrologers fell to his knees and spoke in a halting whisper as he pressed his face against the floor and lay flat before his king. "Our noble king, we fear you will remove our heads if we tell you what the stars predict."

"You will not be punished for telling me what is to be," answered the king.

"Your Majesty, it is written in the stars that your son will . . . will . . ." His trembling voice could not continue.

"On with it, on with it," said the king impatiently.

"It is written in the stars that your son . . . that your son will kill his father," stammered the old astrologer.

The queen fainted. When she regained consciousness, her husband told her that their son was gone forever.

"You killed him?" she asked.

"No, I could not take the life of our handsome baby. I put him in a golden bowl, and at this moment he is floating down the river. We shall never see him again."

The queen wept for many days, and no one, not even the king, was able to console her.

The golden bowl floated down the river, sparkling in the sunshine as it bobbed up and down in the water. The motion of the waves rocked the royal baby to sleep. As he slumbered, the river current carried him out of his father's realm into the small neighboring kingdom of Ratburi.

Most certainly the little prince would have perished if it had not been for an old peasant woman named Yai Hom. As the *phi*, or spirits, would have it, she was tending a flock of ducks on the bank of the river when the glitter of the golden bowl attracted her attention. She left her ducks and waded far out into the river to investigate.

"What is this?" she exclaimed, as she picked up the baby and pressed him to her breast.

"You precious little mouse," she said, "who are you tiny stranger? Where have you come from?"

The wee prince cried loudly and struggled in old Yai Hom's arms. He was hungry, tired, and his delicate golden skin had been burned in the sunlight. Old Yai Hom took the child home and cared for him as if he were her very own. She named her adopted son Paan.

As the many years passed, Prince Paan grew tall and handsome. Yai Hom grew wrinkled and feeble. She never told Prince Paan the mystery of his birth, and the secret grew heavy on her conscience. One day she went to the palace and rang the king's bell on the pavilion. The king heard the toll of the bell and came to answer Yai Hom's request for his advice.

"Old woman, your king will help you, if he is able. Tell me, what brings you to the palace today?"

Yai Hom's eyes filled with tears for she loved Paan and did not want to part with him; yet she managed to tell the king all about that day long ago when Paan had floated down the river in the golden bowl.

"It is a strange story," said the king, "but, I do not doubt your word. I think it is best if you bring the boy to me. I shall educate him and treat him as if he were the son of a king."

From that day onward Paan was brought up as a member of the royal family. He quickly mastered the rituals of court procedure and rapidly learned the special phrases used by the nobility. He was tutored as a prince and learned so rapidly that everyone felt the king had shown exceptionally wise judgment in bringing the boy to court.

When Paan was nineteen years old, the king of Ratburi summoned him to a private conference. "Prince Paan," he said, "I have decided to send you on a special mission to the king of Kanburi. You are asked to present him with our yearly tribute, three artificial trees made of gold and three artificial trees made of silver."

"I shall do as you say, but why do we send all our wealth out of the country?" asked the prince.

"Many years ago I made a truce with the great King Phya Kong. I promised to make this yearly tribute. He promised never to invade Ratburi. Both of us are men of honor, and we have kept our words," explained the king.

The young prince's face scowled, and he clenched his fists as he said, "Your Highness, do not send our gold and silver out of the country. There is no reason to fear an invasion from the great King Phya Kong. If he comes, I shall lead your army to victory."

It is said, the king was reluctant to break the terms of the truce; however, he respected Prince Paan's judgment and declared, "This year the gold and silver trees will remain in Ratburi."

Just as the king of Ratburi suspected, King Phya Kong declared war when the gold and silver trees failed to arrive. The great King Phya Kong rode his most fierce war elephant. He, himself, led his army of warriors to the border of his kingdom where the river flows from Kanburi into Ratburi.

Prince Paan met the great King Phya Kong with a spear in his hand. He showed no fear, but his heart turned over in his chest when he saw the great king.

The king laughed a little and said to himself, "They have sent a boy to do a man's job. That black vest he wears will not help him very much. The color black may terrify some enemies, but it certainly does not frighten me."

All day the two armies fought. When night came, Prince Paan discovered his men had retreated, and he alone remained in battle.

"My men have retreated because your army is greater than mine," shouted the young prince.

King Phya Kong admired the courage of the young man. He could have captured him easily, but instead he said, "Let us finish the battle. You and I shall fight single-handed."

Prince Paan agreed. Just as the sun was setting, the king

led his elephant into the final charge against his son. The elephant lowered its head and aimed its tusks at the side of the enemy elephant. Paan threw his spear. The king ducked beneath it. It seemed as if each man had found his equal, but at just that moment, the king's elephant stumbled. Prince Paan drew his sword and swung it wildly. His sharp blade beheaded the great King Phya Kong. At that moment the earth trembled and the ground opened to receive the head of the king of Kanburi. Just as the astrologers had predicted, Prince Paan killed his father.

The prince was weary and felt no joy. When his army gathered around him shouting, *"Chai-yo! Chai-yo!* Bravo! Bravo!"* the prince was not moved by these words of praise.

"Come," his men shouted to him, "as the victor you may claim the great Phya Kong's queen as your bride."

"I wish no such thing, but I must declare my victory," he answered.

From the palace window the queen watched the prince approach.

"He resembles my husband," she said. "Why, he could be the son of the king." And then she realized what had happened and knew the astrologers' prediction had been fulfilled.

Just as the prince entered the palace, the queen's cats began to snarl and howl. The queen burst into tears. Between her sobs she managed to say, "You killed your father, Paan. Nineteen years ago the great Phya Kong placed you in a golden bowl and allowed you to float away. Today you have returned to me with your father's blood still moist on your clothes. Paan, please go and allow me to weep the tears of a broken-hearted wife and mother."

The prince was dazed and startled, yet he remembered the beautiful golden bowl in old Yai Hom's hut. "Yes, it is true. Every word the queen uttered is true," the prince muttered. "Old Yai Hom should have told me the truth. Ah, she should have let me drown. I have killed my father, the great King Phya Kong. There is no greater crime. I must avenge my father's death, and old Yai Hom must die."

In an effort to escape from guilt, he returned to Ratburi and ordered the killing of the old woman who had raised him as a son.

When the evil deed was done, the prince wandered for seven days and seven nights without food or drink. Weak and exhausted, he collapsed on a jungle trail and was carried to the home of Buddhist priests. They nursed him back to life and tried to strengthen his spirits with their teachings.

"Men of the *sangha*, you must help me," said the prince. "Is there some way I can atone for my horrible crimes?"

"You must build a memorial to your father," said the priests. "You must build a temple with a *chedi* taller than the wild pigeon flies."

"I will find a way to do it," said the prince.

From that moment until his dying day Prince Paan devoted his life to the accomplishment of this mission.

*   *   *

The people of Nakhon Pathom take great pride in the beauty of Thailand's oldest and largest religious structure. They believe the legend of Prince Paan is a true story. If you should visit Nakhon Pathom, the inhabitants will show you a grassy mound of earth, a place called Thanon Kat. It is believed this is where the ground actually opened to receive the head of King Phya Kong. In the shadow of the great Golden Chedi stands a smaller *chedi*. It is said Prince Paan built the second memorial to honor the memory of old Yai Hom.

PART TWO

Thailand and Her People

A Salute to the Kings of Old Siam

Readers of *Tales from Thailand* will ask two questions about this exotic country. Why are so many of the Thai folktales about members of the royal family? When did Siam become Thailand? The answer to both questions will be found as we examine some of the ancient writings that tell us about the kings of old Siam and the founder of the present dynasty.

The king and his family have always been of special interest to the Thai people. This is understandable, for the king was usually the strongest, most intelligent, and most capable man in the tribe. He was a symbol of unity, a father figure who inspired both reverence and respect. The men who were chosen king were capable leaders who had proven their merit on the difficult testing ground of battle. Personal courage and bravery demonstrated in hand-to-hand combat were necessary qualities for a king. The man who possessed them was the kind of man who inspired legends of bravery and cleverness.

The great reverence and honor shown a king came naturally from grateful citizens. They even devised a special court language to honor their ruler with distinctive courtesy phrases. They willingly knelt low and prostrated themselves before their ruler. Yet, they never claimed their king was a god. Their king was a mortal man, like themselves, who had distinguished himself in ways which would bring honor to himself and his people.

The king was always expected to uphold the Buddhist religion and conform to court ritual. Although the religious beliefs were Buddhist, the court rituals were the teachings of Brahman priests, supporters of the old Hindu religion. The ideal or perfect king possessed ten kingly virtues: lack of anger, forbearance, lack of violence, lack of obstruction, self-denial, gentleness, rectitude, liberality, morality, and generosity. Not all kings could meet these high expectations, of course, but it was understood that every king should strive toward this image of the ideal king to the best of his ability.

The story of old Siam and its transition to modern Thailand is a dramatic sequence of historical events featuring the kings of the country. Thailand's monarchs have done more than lead armies; they have guided their country through tense and critical times and provided inspired leadership in politics, commerce, education, social developments, and the arts. The king's place in an accurate account of Thailand can best be understood by literally translating the Thai word for history, *nah prawatsart*. It means the story of kings.

Ancient Chinese chronicles refer to the Thai tribes as "the barbarians beyond the Yangtze." The Thai were fierce warriors and they may have been barbaric according to the Chinese, but they were well organized and had an efficient government in which special officers were appointed to handle the finances, the rice paid in as taxes, the army, palace rituals, and commerce. The early Thai kings were capable administrators who had absolute power over every branch of their government.

The Sukhotai Dynasty

The Great King Rama Kamheng, who ruled from 1275–1315, illustrates some of the characteristics that have inspired the loyalty and devotion of the Thai people. Whenever Rama Kamheng's people needed his advice or assistance, they were permitted to enter the palace courtyard and ring a gigantic bronze bell. It is said that King Kamheng never ignored the tolling of his people's bell. It was King Kamheng who expanded the area of his country to its present boundaries, and it was he who fashioned an alphabet for his people. King Kamheng is best remembered as a champion of justice, but his influence was felt in statesmanship and commerce. He actually sent goodwill ambassadors to the court of the mighty Kublai Khan and may have visited the famous Mongol ruler himself. We do know he traveled to China and persuaded Chinese potters to come to Thailand and teach the people at Sawankhalok the secret arts of making pottery. Kings such as Rama Kamheng inspired loyalty and love for monarch and country. When he led the way, the Thai were willing to battle and die for their country.

Historians call King Kamheng the originator of the Sukhotai dynasty. His descendants ruled from the northern capital city of old Sukhotai until the early fourteenth century. The Sukhotai period came to an end when the daring young Prince Tibodi from the province of U-Thong took control of all Siam.

The Ayudhya Period

Young Rama Tibodi decided to rule from a new capital city, Ayudhya. His choice became a wealthy, prosperous city destined to be the center of all major historical developments for a period of four hundred years. The young King Tibodi gave the Ayudhya period an impressive start with a strict code of laws which brought order and control to the entire nation.

The Ayudhya period is sometimes called the Golden Age of Thailand. It was an exciting period of cultural growth and commercial development. Marco Polo, the first European to enter the realm of the Thai, came long before the Ayudhya period, but several hundred years later a group of Portuguese sailors visited this region. In 1518, the king gave them permission to establish a trading center and start a small mission in the capital.

The kings who ruled during the Ayudhya period from 1350–1767 faced the dangers and problems of war with Burma, Cambodia, and Laos. They also witnessed the growth of international trade to such a point that a special royal officer, Phra Klang, was appointed to handle the Asian and European exports. Ayudhya grew to accommodate over a million people who lived comfortably by the river's edge in their tall houses built on stilts. Even today one can examine ruins that supply evidence of the great wealth and luxury of Ayudhya.

Unfortunately, the Burmese attacked the Thai and plundered Ayudhya in 1767. As a result of repeated attacks, the Burmese taking Thai prisoners, and a series of dreadful epidemics, the Ayudhya population fell from a million to ten thousand. The beautiful capital city with its magnificent palaces and court buildings was reduced to rubble.

The Ayudhya period gave king and commoner numerous opportunities for valor and heroism. The lives they lived were so inspiring that today Thai children memorize the stories of the brave men and women who helped to make the Ayudhya period a time of growth and development.

THE WHITE ELEPHANT WAR

Almost any Thai school boy can describe the White Elephant War of 1563. It is said the king of Burma discovered that King Maha Chakrapat, the ruler of Siam, enjoyed the remarkable prestige of seven white elephants. The Burmese king was furious because in all Burma there was not one white elephant. The white elephant is the legendary symbol of royal power, and the Burmese king was determined to have one at any cost.

The Burmese king demanded three of King Chakrapat's elephants. When King Chakrapat refused, the Burmese king led an army to the beautiful capital city Ayudhya. From the wall of the city King Chakrapat and Queen Suriyothai watched the swarming sea of Burmese soldiers.

"They are more numerous than the leaves of the jungle," said the queen.

"*Mai pen rai,* never mind," said the king. "We will go out and meet them. I want them to attack us, and when they do, we will defeat them."

"I want to go into the battle with you," said the queen.

"No, you must stay in the city where it is safe," answered the king.

The queen was determined, and when the king went into battle, she was at his side. She watched him lead his war elephants into the heat of battle. He was dueling with the Burmese prince when the queen saw her husband's body weave with the sway of his elephant. It was evident that

the king would soon meet his death, but then Queen Suriyothai courageously spurred her elephant between the
elephants of the royal warriors and received the fatal spear
intended for her husband. The great King Maha Chakrapat's life had been spared. He wept for his brave queen,
but did not halt the war. In four months the Burmese were
forced to withdraw their forces. The king of Burma had not
been able to capture a single white elephant.

THE BLACK PRINCE

Another favorite story from the historical Ayudhya
period is about the Black Prince Naresuan who was captured by the Burmese and raised in Rangoon with the
Burmese royal princes. The Black Prince was an intelligent
and inquisitive child who was educated in the art of warfare
by the Burmese. Later, when the Black Prince was a young
man, the Burmese king trusted him to such an extent that
permission was granted for the Black Prince to organize and
train an army composed of captured Thai soldiers. The
prince affectionately referred to his men as Naresuan's
Wild Tigers. The Wild Tigers grew in strength until one
day they succeeded in defeating the Burmese army and
returned triumphantly to Siam.

Soon after this the Black Prince became King Naresuan
of old Siam. His first major challenge was with his former
hosts, the Burmese. An enemy force of two hundred and
fifty thousand Burmese soldiers threatened the border between Siam and Burma. The Black Prince ordered all his
people in the north to withdraw and burn their rice fields
behind them. Thousands of Siamese farmers fled from their
homes and carried their freshly harvested rice to Ayudhya.
The new king set up training camps and turned every able-
bodied man into a soldier.

The war was long and painful to both Burma and Siam, but neither army would give in to the other. Peace finally came one day when King Naresuan's war elephant was accidentally startled and nothing could prevent the animal from running madly into the enemy lines. When the dust from the elephant's hoofs cleared, King Naresuan discovered he was face to face with his enemy, the Burmese crown prince.

King Naresuan was surrounded by a large force of enemy soldiers. The Burmese prince could have ordered his death, but instead he nobly accepted King Naresuan's challenge to a duel. The two fought with spears and swords from the backs of their elephants. When the Burmese prince urged his elephant forward, Naresuan swung his sword and wounded his childhood companion. He died a few moments later. King Naresuan declared an armistice while the Burmese soldiers removed the body of their slain prince from the battlefield. There is no doubt that King Naresuan admired the man he had been forced to kill. On the very site of their personal battle he erected a memorial *chedi* in honor of the slain Burmese prince.

Without their crown prince to lead them, the Burmese had no heart for battle. They withdrew their forces and for a short time the Burmese and the people of Siam enjoyed a period of peace.

*   *   *

Men such as King Naresuan and King Chakrapat are not easily forgotten. A visit to the charred ruins of old Ayudhya revives the memories and stories of old. The Burmese destruction of Ayudhya in 1767 was thorough. All records, archives, and manuscripts were lost in raging fires that turned hand-carved teakwood buildings into

mounds of ashes. The gold and precious gems that decorated the many *wat,* or temples, were stolen when the
Burmese pillaged the city. Some say the destruction of
Ayudhya was so complete that the flutter of a bird's wing
was not seen for three months after the final battle. But the
stories live on, and the Thai will never forget the men who
made the Ayudhya period a Golden Age.

The Thai did not accept the Burmese defeat willingly.
Within ten years after their fall, they had driven the
Burmese beyond their border, re-established their government, and had a new capital city at Thonburi, across the
river from Bangkok. All this was done under the leadership
of General Taksin.

The Chakkri Dynasty

In 1782, General Taksin was put to death by a group of
court officials who claimed he was insane. He was succeeded
by General Chakkri, the founder of the present dynasty.
General Chakkri, better known as Rama I, has achieved
fame as a capable administrator, a gallant soldier, and a
learned scholar who strove to keep alive the Sukhotai and
Ayudhya heritage. He selected the site of the Grand
Palace in Bangkok which is still in use today. Under his
direction Thai literature was recorded, the arts flourished,
and Bangkok as the capital city acquired some of the beauty
and dignity reminiscent of old Ayudhya.

There have been nine rulers in the Chakkri dynasty
since Rama I ascended the throne over two hundred years
ago. Each Chakkri king has succeeded in maintaining pride
in the Thai history and interest in the Thai cultural heritage. Almost miraculously they have kept their country free
of European domination, even when the surrounding
countries fell under European influence.

In 1932, the Thai leaders shifted from an absolute monarchy to a constitutional form of government. *Prachatipitai*, the Thai word for democracy, was on everyone's lips. With the government divided into seventy-one *changwat*, or provinces, plans for electing officials were easily administered. Each person had a dream of contributing to the life and voice of his country. That dream still exists today. The Thai people compromised and accepted autocratic rulers because they deemed it necessary for their safety. Autocratic rule does not seem offensive to the Thai when it perpetuates the constitution, gives honor to a revered king, and permits the free to live as forefathers have lived.

The shift from an absolute monarchy to a constitutional monarchy was the beginning of the country's progress to modern ideas and methods. In 1939 this spirit of modernization was given further impetus with a dramatic change in the name of the country. Siam, the name of the country for six hundred years, was changed to Thailand, which means the Land of the Free.

Since then the Thai have adopted numerous Western ways to improve their schools, health standards, and building methods. In Bangkok Western fashion is often substituted for the traditional Thai dress. Bangkok has wide, paved streets, electricity, television (with "Superman" speaking Thai), newspapers in several languages, and numerous new buildings reflecting the most advanced architectural designs. It is the showplace of Thailand. Four hundred golden-spired *wat* with their enormous Buddhas, the *klong*, floating markets, and the impressive Grand Palace built in the graceful, imaginative Thai style all blend to make Bangkok a most unusual and distinctive city.

The present king of Thailand, King Bhumibol Adulyadej,

was born in Cambridge, Massachusetts. His father was a student of Public Health at the Harvard Medical School. He is the only Thai king who was born in the United States and is the only Thai king who has won fame as a jazz musician and composer. Under the laws of the constitutional monarchy, the king no longer rules; rather, he reigns over his people. He participates in religious festivals, public ceremonies, and numerous civic functions. The king makes tours of the provinces, at times represents his country abroad, and has numerous special duties. An example of this is his privilege of changing the robes of the sacred Emerald Buddha at the onset of each new season. The great variety of his duties can be determined from his full name and title which is: His Majesty the Supreme Divine Lord, Great Strength of the Land, Incomparable Mighty, Greatest in the Realm, Lord Rama, Holder of the Kingdom, Chief of the Sovereign People, Sovereign of Siam, Supreme Protector, and Monarch. Although the king's role is primarily ceremonial, his position and office provide a great assurance to the people. The king and his lovely Queen Sirikit remind the Thai of their long heritage and the traditions of the past. Even today, just as in the distant past, the Thai king is a symbol of Thai unity.

The future of Thailand seems as bright as the tropical sun that blazes over her horizon each day. As the country progresses on its way to modernization and democracy, it is our sincere wish, that it remains Muang Thai, the Land of the Free. The stories of its kings and the folktales of its people present a picture of a confident, capable people who are destined to play a prominent role in the future of Southeast Asia.

Folktales and the Thai Culture

For many hundreds of years the Thai folktales have been told and told again. An important reason for their durability and their popularity lies in their purpose. The stories have helped to bind the people together; at the same time they have given the Thai strength, courage, and faith in themselves.

The early Thai needed courage, faith, and fortitude to cope with their rugged existence. Stories about common men, like the rice farmer Hon Mee who became a hero, made it easier for them to face enemies bravely. The continual dangers of everyday life became less frightening when stories were known about gods who extended a helping hand in time of need. An example of this occurs when the Mother Goddess of the Sea assists Golden Flower, Phikool Thong, who might have perished without supernatural assistance. "Sri of Siam" and other stories about royalty gave the common man an association with his socially distant rulers. The clever plotting of the father-in-law in "The Gold Harvest" is typical of the ingenious and imaginative way the Thai face life. The early Thai who created the

first folktales had courage and a confident approach to the problems of living. Even today this assurance is reflected in their stories.

Another interesting aspect of the Thai folktales is their reflection of the beliefs and practices of the people. Some of the superstitions described in the stories are still followed by the Thai country people. Although ninety-four percent of the Thai are Buddhist, many of them blend their Buddhism with folk beliefs that existed long before Buddha was born.

From reading the stories you learned that the Thai believe in a household spirit, the guardian of their home and compound. His name is Phra Phum. They also believe in a multitude of gods who can fly from heaven to earth, take the shape of man or beast, and even become invisible if they wish. According to folk belief, the gods have great power and great magic.

Besides reflecting Thai beliefs, the stories also give us an opportunity to observe the Thai personality. A concern for helpless creatures and an indication of a gentle nature can be observed in a story from northeastern Thailand explaining the creation of the star constellation known in the Western world as the Pleiades. According to village folk this constellation came into existence one day long ago when six little chicks jumped into a boiling kettle of water to die with their mother. The mother hen had been selected to become chicken curry for the great god Phya Tan. The god recognized the love and the loyalty of the little chicks and gave them eternal life at their mother's side in a constellation of twinkling stars.

Another story tells us what the Thai think of their attractive women. It has been said that a king of the gods, named Setep, once fell in love with a lovely maiden named Madhana. She could not return his love, for her heart belonged to another. The angry Setep responded by turning Madhana into a rose. This is how the rose became the symbol of the delicate beauty and slender grace of the feminine Thai. Since Madhana remained true to her love, the rose is also representative of traits all Thai admire: loyalty and faithfulness.

Some of the stories were selected to reveal the liking the Thai have for colorful festivals, ancient rituals, sports, and games. The Thai are a fun-loving people. They sing and laugh as they work, and they delight in parties, celebrations, and amusements of all kinds. Fish fighting, cock fighting, and kite fighting are popular Thai sports. They also enjoy their own individual form of basketball, golf, and boxing. Many of the sports are outdoor activities because the climate is both mild and tropical.

There is something about sunshine that brightens one's heart and cheers the spirit. Thailand's sun shines through each of its three seasons. There is a hot season, a wet season, and a cool season. The sun's bright glow never departs from Thailand. With this mild climate the Thai are comfortable with light clothing and small, easily constructed huts made from bamboo and palm thatch.

Sometimes the Thai are called a water people. Those who live on the Central Plain deserve the title for they spend almost as much time in the water as they do on land. These people enjoy using a system of canals for transportation and rice irrigation. The *klong*, to use the Thai word for canals, also provide a steady supply of fish, water for drinking, cooking, bathing, washing clothes, and a place for the children to swim. Few Thai families have an automobile, but nearly everyone in central Thailand has a *klong* boat. Children paddle to school, fathers take a *klong* boat to work, and mothers use a *klong* boat to get to the unique floating markets where they can purchase everything they need without getting out of their boats. The *klong* is rarely mentioned in the Thai stories. Perhaps, the reason for this lies in the age of the tales. It is possible the stories were created before the invention of the *klong*.

Because of the *klong* system of transportation many world travelers call Thailand "The Venice of the East." Another name for Thailand is "The Land of Smiles." The latter seems appropriate because the Thai people are friendly, happy, and generous. There are three reasons for this: the climate is agreeable, food is plentiful and inexpensive, and the Thai are a free people.

Thailand's warm climate and fertile soil produce an amazing variety of fruits and vegetables. Thai cooks use them to create a wonderful assortment of tasty dishes. Rice is the main staple of their diet and it is served with fish, fowl, and spicy curries. Of course, tropical fruits and coconut sweets are frequently a part of the menu.

Warmth and good food may produce many smiles, but if you wish to see a really big grin, speak to a Thai about his country. The Thai refer to their homeland as Muang Thai, the Land of the Free. Thailand has never been ruled by a European power, and the Thai are proud of this fact.

Since Malaya, Burma, Laos, and Cambodia, the countries surrounding Thailand, were once under the control of Europe, Thailand's history does seem remarkable.

Geography of Thailand

If you look at a map of Thailand, you will notice that the country resembles the shape of an elephant's head. An ear flops near Burma, and the trunk swings down into Malaya. The country occupies two hundred thousand square miles of rice land, rubber plantations, teak forests, coastal regions, and mountainous areas. It is a small Southeast Asian kingdom, not quite as big as Texas. Thirty-three million people live in this exotic country, and nearly half

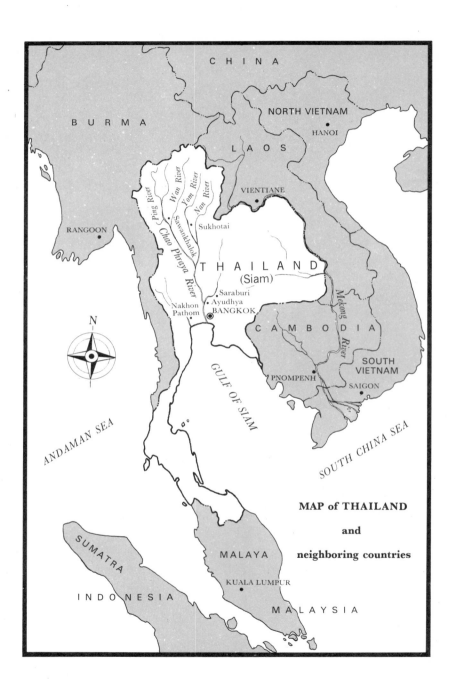

MAP of THAILAND

and

neighboring countries

of them have homes in the Central Plain, the rice basket of Thailand.

The Central Plain has rich farmland created by the constant overflowing of the Chao Phraya River as it carries the black earth deposits to the rice basket region. Here the land is so fertile that enough rice is grown to feed all the people in the country, and there is even enough left over for export to other countries. Sometimes as much as one hundred and fifty million dollars' worth of rice is exported in a single year. Farming is the main occupation in Thailand, and rice is the most important crop.

North of the rice fields there are hills and small mountains. Many primitive tribes live in this area. They are the Shawn, Meow, Karen, Yao, and other tribes that are not as numerous, such as a most unusual group of people who call themselves the Spirits of the Yellow Leaves. Few Westerners have seen these people, for they have no permanent home. They wander from place to place eating wild fruits, herbs, and roots.

Since the northern part of Thailand is rich with teak and rosewood forests, the principal industry is forestry. This area is so dense with vegetation that it is impossible to use

modern methods of forestry, but the Thai have solved this problem by training elephants to do the work. Elephants pull teak logs and push them into the rivers that flow south to the lumber mills.

The southern part of Thailand, the trunk of the elephant, extends into the Malay Peninsula. This part of the country is green jungle land, yet parts of it are slightly mountainous. The southern area is rich with tin deposits and numerous, prosperous rubber plantations.

The geography of the country is the subject of several Thai legends. Stories about the creation of the Bay of Siam and the Mekong River are in this book.

Origins of the People

The facts on origins of the Thai people are almost as interesting. Historians tell us that many centuries ago the

Thai lived in the valleys of northwestern China. They had their own language and their own customs, but they did come in contact with other cultures when they intermarried with the Mongols and the Chinese. We know that as early as 233 B.C., the Thai left China and traveled south in their search of independence and freedom. Numerous conflicts with Mongol and Chinese lords sent them further southward until they found the fertile valleys and the rich lands of what is known today as the Central Plain.

The Thai found two other groups of people living there: the Khmer and the Mon. The Thai lived side by side with them, and there was no major conflict until A.D. 1050. That year the Burmese King Anuruddha attacked the Khmer. The Thai helped the Khmer drive the Burmese out of the land. From that time onward the Thai gradually took control of the land from the Khmer. During the difficult years that followed the Thai gradually shaped a kingdom extending from the mountains in the north to the rich Central Plain and south to the jungle land of the Malay Peninsula.

The Thai people existed long before the historical records, however. In the story about Phya Tan's fire festival the children of the gods came to earth and became the earliest ancestors of the Thai. This story is told by the tribes who live in the north along the banks of the Mekong River.

The Thai tell how-it-came-to-be stories frequently as explanations for things that are rather difficult to understand. An example of this kind of story was told to me once when I asked why the Beuk fish are found only in the Mekong River.

My Thai friend answered: "Once, long ago, the rivers of Thailand had a race to see which one could flow the most rapidly. The little rivers visited and chatted merrily together, but the Mekong flowed steadily on its way, never stopping until it reached the China Sea. The Mekong's prize for this achievement was the honor of providing a home for the Beuk fish."

Near Larnchang I asked a Thai friend why the white orchid always grows near the lavender orchid. In response I was told a beautiful love story about Nang Hawa and Prince Kuloo who died a tragic death. Their love, however, was so true that the gods gave them eternal life as flowers. For this reason one always sees the delicate, lavender Nang Hawa and the fragile, white Kuloo orchids together.

The sun was setting as I became aware of a sweet, fragrant perfume. My Thai friend explained: "Between sunset and the break of day the orchids release this scent. The flowers smell sweetly because this is the time of day when Prince Kuloo called upon his beloved Nang Hawa."

Animals and Birdlife

Stories about the rivers and flowers of Thailand are a reflection of the people. Since this is true, our image of the Thai will be completely out of focus if we do not mention their animals and birdlife. Elephants, monkeys, crocodiles, water buffalo, bears, deer, tigers, and reptiles of all kinds wander from the jungles, forests, and farmlands of Thailand into the folk literature of the people.

Of all these animals, the Thai elephant receives the most regard. We have already noted that the shape of Thailand resembles an elephant's head. A stay in Thailand also tells us that many places are honored with the elephant's name. There is Ban Chang Lek, or Little Elephant Village; Khao Chang, or Elephant Mountain; Khuan Chang, or Elephant Hill; Ko Chang, or Elephant Island; Nam Mai

Chang, or Elephant River, and Non Hua Chang, or Elephant Head Marsh.

Naming an area after the elephant is an honor to the species; however, the highest tribute ever paid to the elephant came from Buddha. The well-known Buddha birth stories reveal that Buddha is believed to have lived an earlier life as an elephant.

Elephants have played a prominent place in Thai history. The white elephant is a prized possession in Southeast Asia. Whenever one is captured, it is immediately presented to the king. The discovery of a white elephant at any time prompts a festive holiday; however, there are special, national celebrations if one is found at the beginning of a new king's reign. The Thai regard the white elephant as an auspicious omen of great prosperity and unusual good fortune. White elephants live in elaborate luxury and do nothing for their keep except participate in parades and festivals.

The life of a working elephant is quite different. He labors approximately five hours each day. They are directed by skillful trainers who began preparing for their professions in childhood. Actually, the elephant trainer is raised with the same elephants he will manage in later life. He knows his elephants as well as he knows the members of his family. He is even able to communicate with them by using a common elephant language. The elephants are unusually intelligent and easily learn to respond to their trainer's gestures and words.

Evidence of the elephant's past prominence can be seen near the old ruins of the ancient capital Ayudhya. The Ayudhya corral made from sturdy teak pillars reminds us of days long past when Thai kings kept hundreds of elephants in captivity. Royalty rode upon them in decorated splendor. The ranking soldiers used to go to war upon the elephants' backs. The huge animals were also used then, just as they are employed today, as a powerful work force.

Not every Thai has an elephant, but nearly every Thai farmer has at least one water buffalo to help him plow and work his rice paddy. The buffalo is a valuable animal, and he is rarely left alone. Usually a farmer's son guards the buffalo when the animal is not working. It is a common sight to see a little boy wearing nothing except a smile as he comfortably rests on the broad back of his father's buffalo.

In the late afternoon, when the work in the paddy is over, the rice farmer removes the yoke from the buffalo and climbs upon his back. He takes his bamboo flute from his

pocket and plays a merry melody as· the buffalo jerkily trods homeward. This time of the day is called "buffalo afternoon."

The monkeys in Thailand are not as useful as the water buffaloes, but one species, the pigtailed monkey, does perform a service for his masters. In the southern part of Thailand clever workers have trained this monkey to pick both fruit and coconuts. His Thai cousins, the Java, Stumptail, Rhesus, Langur, and Sawart Macacques, are playful fellows, not workers.

Monkeys and gibbons are often kept as household pets. Readers of this book have discovered why the gibbon ape says *pua*. No explanation has ever been given for his affectionate, clownish instincts.

Biologist know Thailand as a realm of reptiles. At least thirty varieties of snakes slither in the grass, swim in the ponds, and dangle from the tropical trees. Turtles of numerous sizes and shapes splash in the *klong* and streams. Occasionally one sees the hated giant *hia* lizard and worries about the bad luck he is supposed to bring. Myriads of little *chingchok* scamper over the walls of homes and office buildings looking for mosquitoes. Geckos, larger sized lizards, croak in the gardens predicting good luck. Iguanas bask in the ever-present sunshine. Crocodiles inhabit the rivers and marshlands.

Eleven species of Thailand's snakes are poisonous, and among them, the cobra is by far the most dangerous. The cobra is able to shoot his deadly venom and blind a person from a distance of three feet. The Thai seldom deliberately kill an animal because of the Buddhist respect for life; however, the farmers do kill cobras, and they carefully burn the body to prevent the spirit of the snake from returning to bite them. Some Chinese who live in Bangkok sell the cobra's spleen for medicinal purposes. They also believe that a soup made from the cobra meat will improve one's eyesight.

All *farang*, or foreigners, fear the crocodiles that bask on the banks of the rivers and swim in the swamps and marshlands of Thailand. The largest member of the Thai crocodile family lives in the tidal waters of the rivers. He is the killer of his species and has been known to attack humans while they were bathing. This crocodile lives as long as seventy years and grows to a huge weight of nine hundred pounds. Fresh-water crocodiles live in the northern part of Thailand; slender-snouted crocodiles reside in the south.

"Du ari?" means "What are you looking at?" It is a phrase often asked the *farang* who are fascinated with Thailand's colorful birds. In Thailand there are almost as many birds in the sky as there are flowers on the land. Birdsongs echo and birdcalls create lovely music throughout the entire country, reminding one of flutes and piccolos with a new range of tone.

Thai stories reflect a sincere interest in birdlife. One story in this collection explains why the crow is black. Another story from India tells how two little ricebirds found happiness in a later life when they were reborn as people. This story was included to illustrate the Thai Buddhist belief in reincarnation. It also illustrates the belief in the idea that a person's last dying thought will influence his later life.

"The Lorikeet and Man," another bird story, explains why the parrot echoes man's words. It is a very short story that goes like this:

One day Man found a beautiful bird called Lorikeet. It was the most unusual bird he had ever seen. Its feathers were like the colors of the wild jungle flowers. Man brought the new bird into his home because it was so lovely, and he was thrilled to discover that the bird was as talented as it was beautiful. The Lorikeet was able to speak to Man in Man's own language.

One day after the Lorikeet moved into Man's house, Man killed his neighbor's water buffalo. When he was questioned about the missing animal, Man said, "I did not do it."

The Lorikeet knew better. He said, "Man does not tell what really happened."

Everyone listened to the Lorikeet, and because they believed him, it was decided to send for the village headman and give Man a trial.

The night before the trial guilty Man covered his Lorikeet's cage with an iron cooking pot. All during the night he splashed water on the pot so that the Lorikeet would think a terrible rainstorm fell from the sky.

The next day Man, his Lorikeet, all the neighbors, and the village headman gathered for the trial.

"You are accused of killing your neighbor's buffalo," said the headman.

Before Man could answer the Lorikeet said, "He stole it, killed it, and ate it!"

"Don't believe the Lorikeet," said guilty Man. "He tells stories. Just ask the Lorikeet about the weather last night."

"Well, what kind of weather did we have last evening?"

"It rained and rained all night long," said the Lorikeet.

Man jumped to his feet. "See how he lies! Would you condemn me on his word?"

Guilty Man was allowed to go free. As soon as he was alone with his Lorikeet, he opened the door and said, "Go, fly away and never come back."

Not long after that the lonely Lorikeet met a parrot.

"You have beautiful feathers, and you speak Man's language. More likely than not you will be invited to live in Man's house. If you like it there and want to stay, remember this, Man likes to hear the echo of his own words."

Just as the Lorikeet predicted, the parrot was invited to live in Man's house. He liked it there, and he did not wish to offend his host in any way. The parrot soon realized that Man liked the sound of his own words. Parrots have been mimicking Man from that day to this.

Birds are popular household pets in Thailand, and the Thai have an equal regard for dogs, cats, monkeys, and gibbons. A Buddhist respect for animal life prompts the Thai to care for all stray creatures. Animals are rarely left alone and homeless. When the Thai see a stray animal, they pick it up and take it to the nearest *wat*. There a kind Buddhist priest will provide shelter, food, and medical care if it is needed. Wat Sam Plern in Bangkok is a recognized shelter for all stray crocodiles. A few blocks down the street from this *wat* there is another that provides a home for all stray turtles.

Religious Influences in Thailand

The most colorful buildings in Thailand are the Buddhist temples called *wat*. The towering golden spires, the tinkling bronze bells hanging from the rafters, and the glistening tiles of the gracefully slanting roofs make Thailand's houses of worship enchanting and distinctive.

The *wat* is the heart of Thai village life. It buzzes with activity from the moment the sun's first rays strike the golden roofs until the glass tiles reflect the last glow of sunset. Over half of the government's primary schools are located in the temples. The young children skip into the courtyard looking crisp and clean in their freshly starched, blue-and-white uniforms. Their parents come to place freshly cut flowers and burning incense on the altar before the large gleaming bronze statue of Buddha. Villagers come to ask the priests' advice on personal or business affairs. Housewives pause in the courtyard to relay the local gossip. An elderly man may rest in the shade of his *wat*. If it is Wan Phra, Buddhist Sunday, the *wat* will be full of attentive listeners seated on the floor while hearing a priest's lesson or sermon.

Buddhism is a philosophy that tries to explain the nature of life and the reason for the existence of a universe. It provides a code of personal honor and encourages men to live simply, with noble thoughts and admirable virtues.

The Buddhist religion exerts the strongest force on Thai ideals. It influences the Thai in establishing personal standards, in their relations with one another, and in their personal goals for happiness.

The most fundamental teachings of Buddha encourage each person to seek for peace and perfection just as the great teacher Buddha sought for personal enlightenment. Each Thai child finds daily encouragement in his religious pursuits. Parents try to inspire Buddhist beliefs, and religious instruction is an important course in every school.

Buddha

In order to understand the gracious Thai people, it is necessary to know about Buddha. His teachings have become so much a part of Thailand that they are an integral part of cultural expressions and dominate individual customs of personal life. Ninety-four percent of the Thai are Buddhist. Some of them regard Buddha as a god, but Buddha thought of himself as a teacher. He encouraged his followers to lead a virtuous life by adhering to the Eightfold Path. This is a personal code of behavior that inspires right contemplation, right understanding, right purpose, right speech, right action, right concentration, right effort, and responsiveness to truth.

If a person is able to do all this, he will eventually escape from personal sadness and be well on the way toward becoming enlightened.

An enlightened person enters Nirvana, the Buddhist

heaven, but he must live numerous lives in order to get there. The Thai children usually begin by learning a set of moral rules called the Five Moral Precepts. They prohibit killing, lying, stealing, becoming intoxicated, and the breaking of marriage vows. This Buddhist moral code closely resembles the Christian Ten Commandments.

Buddha taught that it was necessary for man to acknowledge noble truths and principles. He felt man's never-ending desires caused his suffering. If man could realize that he was just a tiny fragment of life in the universe and look beyond his personal desires, he might attain true happiness. Buddha's teachings claim that life never ends until one reaches Nirvana. A man might be reborn as an insect, a fish, an animal, or another man. What a man will be in his next life is decided by an individual power called karma. The total sum of a man's evil or goodness assembled from all his many lives determines the force of his karma.

Gautama Siddhartha, the founder of Buddhism, was born in 543 B.C. His father was the wealthy ruler of a kingdom located in India at the foot of the Himalaya Mountains. Siddhartha was raised in an atmosphere of extravagant wealth. When he was twenty-nine years old, he rejected the regal splendor of his father's palace and concentrated upon the poverty and suffering of the people. He left his wife and children at the palace, gave up all claim to wealth, and became a hermit.

One day Prince Siddhartha sat meditating beneath the bodhi tree in the temple grounds. While concentrating, he experienced enlightenment and found the way to lead men to self-perfection. It is believed his plan for the Eightfold Path was conceived at that time.

The disciples of the prince called him Buddha, the enlightened one. They followed him all over India and helped him teach the Noble Truths and Principles. Some people believe Buddha came to Thailand because his footprint is located at Saraburi. Others say Buddha could not have traveled so far.

Hinduism was the most prominent religion in India during Buddha's lifetime, yet Buddha taught thousands of people to accept his beliefs. After he died, powerful Indian kings sent missionaries to all parts of Southeast Asia including the area that is now Thailand.

According to sacred scriptures written in an ancient language called Pali, Buddha died when he was eighty years old. He had lived a life of noble virtue. The ancient Pali scriptures recorded on palm leaves tell us he entered Nirvana at the conclusion of his life on earth.

No one knows for certain where Buddhism began in Thailand, although some believe the first Indian Buddhist missionaries lived in the town of Nakhon Pathom, located thirty-five miles from Bangkok.

Religious Customs and Beliefs

The people of Thailand modified and adapted various cults and beliefs to their surroundings. In this way they have retained some very old and primitive practices. The Thai still celebrate some Hindu holidays and observe some of the old Brahmanic teachings. They also adhere to some customs of animism, the belief that spirits exist in inanimate things.

Although the great majority of the Thai people are Buddhist, several other religions do exist in Thailand. European and American Christian missionary families have converted approximately eighty thousand Thai citizens to Christianity. Small numbers of Moslems, Hindus, and Chinese followers of Confucius worship in complete freedom.

It is difficult to classify the position of the astrologer in Thailand. He enjoys a position of respect, and there is an astrologers' association that sets national standards. The royal astrologer determines the exact date and time for all important ceremonies. Private citizens consult their own astrologer's advice on numerous personal matters, including the most favorable day for marriage, journeys, parties, funerals, and the best time to plant crops. Sometimes a Buddhist priest is a skilled astrologer.

A few Thai customs, however, have nothing to do with Buddhism. They are a holdover from the Chinese and Indian influences that dominated the country prior to the time of Buddha. An example of Chinese associations is the Thai spirit house. Almost every Thai home and business establishment has a spirit house perched on a pole in the front yard. This little ornate gold and green structure houses Phra Phum, the spirit of the place. Every day incense sticks and flowers are presented to Phra Phum. No one dares offend him because he can cause bad dreams, influence one's prosperity, and bring evil spirits to haunt and tease.

The Tam Kwan is another practice that is not Buddhist. When a person has been ill or away on a long journey, the spirit in his head, the *kwan,* is honored with a gay party. Selected foods are given to the honored one and special music is played. At this time spontaneous poetry and prose is recited in honor of the guest.

It is believed each person has his own spirit or *kwan* in his head. No one should ever touch a Thai person on the head, or point one's toe at the head, or sit towering over the head of a guest. All these actions are considered to be extremely rude and ill mannered.

The Thai vary in their observance of Buddhism. Some hand gifts to the priests, others make regular visits to the *wat*, and nearly all observe the religious holidays. All these practices earn merit for the person who participates. Long ago the very wealthy people built temples to gain merit. There are numerous *wat* now, however, and this practice is no longer encouraged. All Buddhists accept the responsibility of keeping fresh flowers on the altars in the *wat*, and everyone tries to apply some gold leaf to the statues of Buddha. It is known that the average Thai Buddhist is generous with his personal earnings. He gives from five to ten percent of his money to his local *wat*. This does not include the food he may give to the priests each day.

The exact date of religious holidays varies in Thailand. One day each week is Wan Phra, Buddhist Sunday. It can be on any day of the week. The *wat* are open at all times, but a special effort is made to go on Wan Phra day.

All Thai appear to enjoy Kathin Day. It is celebrated when the rains have stopped and the rice fields have been plowed. It is a day for honoring the priests. The king's royal barge floats down the Chao Phraya River to Wat Arun, carrying his personal gifts to the priests. The common people celebrate Kathin by giving new golden robes and special foods to the priests in their village *wat*.

Buddha's enlightenment is celebrated on Visaka Bucha Day in May. Later, when the rice harvests have been completed, numerous pilgrimages are made to the Footprint of Buddha at Saraburi, and to the Golden Pagoda of Nakhon Pathom. All these occasions are festive religious celebrations marked with colorful rituals and distinctive traditions.

The Sangha

Approximately one hundred and fifty thousand men wear the golden, flowing robes of the *bhikku*, or priests. The brotherhood of the *bhikku* is called the *sangha*. The novices who are preparing to enter the priesthood usually number eighty-five thousand. They are called *samanera*. These numbers may seem unusually large for a small country like Thailand. Every young man, however, spends at least three months of his life in the Buddhist *wat* and many elect to stay for several years.

Each morning, as dawn's first rays lighten the sky, Buddhist priests stream from their *wat* with their food bowls under their left arm. They wander into the courtyards of homes and receive offerings of food. The householder always thanks the *bhikku* for the privilege of serving him.

The priests live quite simply in their small one-room cells. They eat just one meal each day and never take any food after twelve o'clock. During the rainy season, sometimes called the Buddhist lent, they spend most of their time in meditation and study. Long ago the priest was also the social worker, the teacher, and the doctor. Today he still teaches and helps the people in numerous ways. Some members of the *sangha* become experts in science, philosophy, or languages. Those who excel receive promotions similar to those in the Christian ecclesiastical system. The life of the priest, or *bhikku,* is not easy. His religion requires him to obey two hundred commandments contained in a written code of monastic discipline called the Patimokkha.

Religious Legends

There are three religious stories in this collection of Thai tales. These stories are known and loved by every child, who learns them by heart and proudly recites them to grandparents. The stories are about Thailand's most treasured religious possessions, the Emerald Buddha, the Footprint of Buddha, and the great Golden Pagoda of Nakhon Pathom. The value of these sacred objects cannot be expressed in dollars, old Thai *tical,* or contemporary Thai *baht.* They are valued beyond money; they are treasures of the heart. The shrine honoring the Footprint of Buddha was duplicated for all the world to see at the Thai pavilion of the New York World's Fair in 1965–66. The story about the Golden Pagoda is rather sad and frightening, yet folklorists in all parts of the world will be interested in this tale because it resembles the great Greek tragedy, "Oedipus the King," by Sophocles.

Buddha was one of the world's most impressive teachers. His moral code reminds us of Moses and his parables remind us of Jesus. He was a kind man who loved all living creatures, even those that failed him. It is interesting to observe how these characteristics are illuminated by Buddha's actions in an old tale that is popular in Southeast Asia.

BUDDHA AND THE TURTLE

Once the turtle was the most honored of all creatures, for he was allowed to be close to Buddha all day and all night. The turtle was permitted to hold the folds of the robes of Buddha. Like a living brooch, he rested on Buddha's chest.

One day a snake engaged the turtle in conversation. The turtle became so interested that he forgot his duty. While answering the snake, he released his grasp. Buddha's robes flew open and the turtle fell to the ground.

The turtle fell on sharp stones and hurt himself badly. Buddha noticed this and said, "Little Turtle, you have neglected your duty. No longer may you travel with me and hold my robes. Yet, I do not wish you harm. Forever more you shall crawl upon the ground, and, to protect you from all injury, I shall give you a sturdy coat."

That is how the turtle got his shell.

Many stone and bronze statues of Buddha represent a man with a most elaborate headdress. His hair appears to be in tight ringlets fastened close to his head. The Indians and some of the Thai people say the ringlets are not curls of hair; the coils represent loving little snails who have gathered to protect their beloved Buddha's head from the hot rays of the sun.

In Southeast Asia there are hundreds of *wat* and thousands of statues bearing a likeness to Buddha. The statue that is most treasured is the Emerald Buddha of Wat Pra Keo in Bangkok. In order that you might appreciate the value of the Emerald Buddha, I would like to share a story with you. The following anecdote was told to me by a Thai teacher one day when I visited the Bangkok College of Education.

THE HEART OF THAILAND

It is said that many years ago a king of Thailand granted an audience to a departing statesman.

He said, "Since you are leaving our country, I would like you to have a souvenir to remind you of Siam. You may select anything you wish."

The statesman did not pause or ponder. He said, "Your Highness, since you have been so generous, I shall ask for the Emerald Buddha of Wat Pra Keo."

The king smiled weakly and replied, "It is yours."

Then the statesman said, "When I return to my country, my king will be most honored when I present him with the Emerald Buddha. He will direct me to select a gift for you. What would you like from my country?"

The king answered, "There is only one thing I desire. Please, give the Emerald Buddha back to me. It is the heart of my country."

The Emerald Buddha is a small statue twenty-three inches high. According to folk belief it was created hundreds of years ago by a god from a precious block of jasper jade. Today it sits under a protective canopy on a tall pedestal richly decorated with gold leaf. On either side of the Emerald Buddha are two sparkling glass balls representing the sun and the moon. Wat Pra Keo, adjacent to the Grand Palace in Bangkok, was erected specifically in honor of the Emerald Buddha.

As the heart of Thailand, the Emerald Buddha receives

the offerings of kings, royalty, and commoners. All may worship at the base of the statue's pedestal, but only the king may touch the jade image of Buddha. Three times a year, at the beginning of the rainy season, the cool season, and the dry season, the king adorns the statue with delicate golden garments decorated with twinkling precious jewels.

An accurate account of the Emerald Buddha's history can be traced from the year 1434. Before that time, however, reality blurs into the mists, and we have only the words of ancestors to explain the creation of the Emerald Buddha.

*　　*　　*

Some day, readers of this book may travel to the exotic city of Bangkok and visit the Emerald Buddha. In the outer courtyard of Wat Pra Keo they will slip off their shoes, and their bare feet will touch the cold stone steps leading to the sculptured entrance of the temple. Within, the air will be filled with the fragrance of jasmine and puffs of sweet incense. Through the slated sunlight they will see the "Heart of Thailand," resplendent in a gown of jewels.

The Thai will welcome my readers graciously with a *wai* and a *sawaddi*. The palms of the hands placed together, the slight bow, and the melodic word form an expression of greeting and farewell. *Sawaddi* means both "hello" and "good-by." At the same time it hints of much more. It suggests, "I am honored to be with you" or "I am pleased to have been in your honorable presence."

I hope my readers will visit Thailand, the land of smiles, tinkling bells, and golden spires. I would like to meet my readers in Bangkok, by the red giant swing, perhaps. Then, in that dream country so far away, I would greet them, just as I shall leave them now, with a *wai* and a sincere *sawaddi*.

Glossary

baht: modern Thai coin that is worth approximately five cents

bhikku: a Thai Buddhist priest

chai: yes, that is right

chai yo: bravo! an exclamation of intense praise

changwat: a political division used for government administration. Thailand is divided into seventy-one provinces, or *changwat.*

chedi: a tall, spired tower serving as a tomb or memorial

chingchok: a small lizard found in Southeast Asia

chula: the name given to the male kite in the Thai sport of kite fighting. The *chula* is a large, star-shaped kite with five points. It is flown on a long string.

du ari: what are you looking at?

farang: foreigner

gingekow: the dinner hour or meal time

hia: a very large lizard that lives in the *klong* and swamps of Thailand

Kathin: a holiday honoring Buddhist priests, held after the rainy season and the plowing of the rice fields

khop khun krap: thank you

klong: canals that serve as water roads, providing arteries for travel and transportation in cities and in the countryside

kwan: the personal spirit residing in the head; a being responsible for health, wealth, and general comfort

lakon: a group of classical Thai dancers

Loy Kathong: a holiday celebrated to appease the spirits of the waters with offerings of food, flowers, incense, clay figures, and lighted candles that are placed in tiny leaf boats that float down the *klong*, streams, and rivers to the sea

mai chai: no, that is not right

mai pen rai: never mind, it does not matter

mai ruu: I do not know

mali: a fragrant flower

Muang Thai: Land of the Free. When the Thai tribes migrated southward from China, they established small communities where Thai was spoken and Thai customs were observed. These communities were called Muang Thai. "Muang" means land, "Thai" means free.

nah prawatsart: history

namprick: a pungent, spicy sauce made from a carefully blended mixture of seasonings, water, and a small, black beetle, which the Thai call *maengda*

pai: go now

pakpao: the name given to the female kite in the Thai sport of kite fighting. The *pakpao* is a small, dainty kite with a long tail. It is frequently made in the shape of a diamond.

phi: spirit

phra: an honorary title meaning "sacred one" or "honored one"

Phra Phum: the sacred spirit of a Thai dwelling called "the spirit of the place"

phutsa: a plum with a delicate, delicious flavor, usually served with a sprinkling of sugar

prachatipitai: democracy

pua: the sound made by the gibbon, and also a word for husband *pung:* a small honey bee which makes its nest and beehive in the forest

ramwong: a graceful Thai folk dance
rawang: careful, watch what you are doing; observe closely

samanera: a novice priest
sangha: the Thai Buddhist brotherhood of priests
sawaddi: hello, how do you do; good-by
Songkran: the New Year's festival

Tam Kwan: a holiday celebrating the return of a loved one or a
    member of the family
tical: an ancient Thai monetary unit

Visaka Bucha: a holiday celebrating Buddha's enlightenment

wai: a Thai greeting made by bringing the palms of the hands together
    and placing the tips of the fingers at the forehead or beneath the
    chin, depending upon the degree of respect one wishes to convey
Wan Phra: a day of the week devoted to religious observances
wat: a Buddhist temple